T0318719

CAMBRIDGE
UNIVERSITY PRESS

Shaftesbury Road, Cambridge CB2 8EA, United Kingdom

One Liberty Plaza, 20th Floor, New York, NY 10006, USA

477 Williamstown Road, Port Melbourne, VIC 3207, Australia

314–321, 3rd Floor, Plot 3, Splendor Forum, Jasola District Centre,
New Delhi – 110025, India

103 Penang Road, #05–06/07, Visioncrest Commercial, Singapore 238467

Cambridge University Press is part of Cambridge University Press & Assessment,
a department of the University of Cambridge.

We share the University's mission to contribute to society through the pursuit of
education, learning and research at the highest international levels of excellence.

www.cambridge.org
Information on this title: www.cambridge.org/9781009298100

DOI: 10.1017/9781009298148

First published 2024

A catalogue record for this publication is available from the British Library

ISBN 978-1-009-29810-0 Paperback
ISSN 2516-0117 (online)
ISSN 2516-0109 (print)

Cambridge Elements ≡

Elements in Shakespeare Performance
edited by
W. B. Worthen
Barnard College

EARLY MODERN MEDIA ECOLOGY

Peter W. Marx
University of Cologne

CAMBRIDGE
UNIVERSITY PRESS

Early Modern Media Ecology

Elements in Shakespeare Performance

DOI: 10.1017/9781009298148
First published online: January 2024

Peter W. Marx
University of Cologne

Author for correspondence: Peter W. Marx, marxp@uni-koeln.de

ABSTRACT: The early modern world was as enigmatic as it was dynamic. New epistemologies and technologies, open controversies about the world and afterworld, encounters with various cultures, and numerous forms of entertainment wetted the appetite for ever-new sensational experiences, an emerging visual language, and different social constellations. Thaumaturgy, the art of making wonder, was the historical term under which many of these forms were subsumed: encompassing everything from magic lanterns to puppets to fireworks, and deliberately mingling the spheres of commercial entertainment, art, and religion. But thaumaturgy was not just an idle pastime but a vital field of cultural and intercultural negotiation. This Element introduces this field and suggests a new form of historiography – media ecology – which focuses on connections, formations, and transformations and takes a global perspective.

KEYWORDS: media ecology, magic lantern, peep box, pre-cinema, Athanasius Kircher

ISBNs: 9781009298100 (PB), 9781009298148 (OC)
ISSNs: 2516-0117 (online), 2516-0109 (print)

Contents

Prologue: "A Most Rare Vision"

Imagine entering a room. As you're blinking from the stark contrast between the bright sunshine outside and the comparably dark chamber, your gaze hits the opposite wall. You recognize yourself, but then there is a rumbling sound and the vision blurs. The image in the mirror vanishes, changes ... a vulture, an ox, an ass appear. A vision, a dream, a trick? Bottom's stumbling words come to mind:

> I have had a most rare vision. I have had a dream, past the
> wit of man to say what dream it was. Man is but an ass if he
> go about to expound this dream. Methought I was – there is
> no man can tell what. Methought I was – and methought
> I had – but man is but a patched fool if he will offer to say
> what methought I had. The eye of man hath not heard, the
> ear of man hath not seen, man's hand is not able to taste, his
> tongue to conceive, nor his heart to report, what my dream
> was. (*Midsummer Night's Dream* IV.1.203–13)

Bottom's stammering mimics Saint Paul's letter to the Corinthians (1 Cor. 2:9), comparing Paul's vision of God with his very earthly experience. But this is not Bottom's vision, and the dark chamber that holds the mirror is not the "Woods near Athens." This is an artificial space, a mixture of laboratory and theatre, designed or rather envisioned by Jesuit Athanasius Kircher (1602–80) in his legendary *Ars Magna Lucis et Umbræ* (*The Great Art of Light and Shadow*, 2nd ed, 1671) (Figure 1). Kircher's machine is meant to provide the experience of a metamorphosis, an existential transformation: from man to animal. Kircher (1671: 782b) himself invokes the myth of the metamorphosis as an individual sensation: "*qua homo se in aliquot animal conversum putet*" (a machine through which man believes to be turned into any optional animal).

Since Greco-Roman antiquity, the fantasy of shape-shifting, voluntarily or involuntarily, has haunted the European imagination – fueled and stirred by Ovid and Apuleius. But Kircher's attempt to create the sensation of a metamorphosis is more than the fulfillment of an ancient myth. It is an attempt to defend scholars like cryptographer and occultist Johannes

Figure 1 *Machina catoptrica*, transformation machine. In: A. Kircher, Amsterdam, 2nd ed., 1671, *Ars Magna Lucis et Umbræ*, p. 783. Permission of Theaterwissenschaftliche Sammlung University of Cologne/Sammlung Werner Nekes (joint ownership: University of Cologne/DFF/Filmmuseum Potsdam).

Trithemius (1462–1516), who had been accused of "artibus diabolicis" (diabolic arts) (Kircher 1671: 782b). Thus, the metamorphosis machine is utopian and sobering at the same time – providing a sensual, potentially transgressive experience while laying open the mundane, mechanical foundation: it is sublime and embarrassing, an eye-opening phenomenon and yet mere prestidigitation.

The scene of this metamorphosis machine can be read as a primal scene of early modern media ecology: it is embedded as much in the emerging discourse of modern physics and sciences (not the least through the idea of the *experiment*) as in the humanist "rediscovery" of antiquity as well as of the Roman Catholic Church's cosmology. It is the materialized form of what Aby Warburg (2010, 427) has described as a *Denkraum* (space of thought): a playing field in which old, new, residual, and newly formatted epistemologies are arranged and rearranged. As Warburg has repeatedly insisted, what might look to us like a schizophrenic juxtaposition of ideas and concepts might be indicative of the transformational constitution of the period.

In this sense, we should pay attention to the voice behind the scene: Athanasius Kircher, SJ, often hailed as one of the last polymaths, occupied many of the intellectual crossroads in this period. Positioning himself alongside scholars like Albert the Great (c. 1200–80) or Trithemius, he accumulated knowledge from all available sources, both in his *Musæum Kircherianum* and in his numerous books (Sepibus 1678; Godwin 2009). But Kircher was a man of the church. His insights and inventions were intended to propel faith and foster the cause of the Roman Catholic Church: the flickering light of the *Laterna Magica* (magic lantern, Figure 2), lavishly presented in his *Ars Magna Lucis et Umbræ*, showed souls in purgatory, illustrating in detail what Hamlet's father is allowed only to hint at: "But that I am forbid / To tell the secrets of my prison-house, / I could a tale unfold whose lightest word / Would harrow up thy soul, freeze thy young blood" (*Hamlet* I.5.13–16).

In all its ambivalence, Kircher's metamorphosis apparatus is more than an obsolete toy of media history. It turns our attention to the complexities and contradictions of the early modern period's obsession with various forms of representation; its insatiable appetite for titillations of all kinds; and its intellectual horizon, which comprises the emergence of rationalism as much as various, conflicting theological models, along with the experience of a cultural contingency that is not yet molded by the idea of Western supremacy.[1] But Kircher is not conducting a mere thought experiment. He insists on the material reality of the apparatus:

[1] Jürgen Osterhammel (2018) has argued convincingly that the idea of Western "supremacy" did not emerge before the eighteenth century.

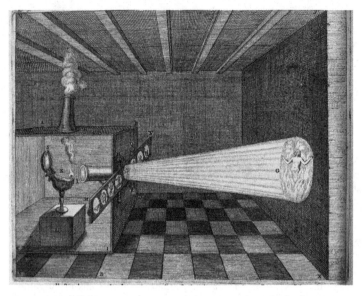

Figure 2 Magic lantern. In: A. Kircher, Amsterdam, 2nd ed., 1671, *Ars Magna Lucis et Umbræ*, p. 768. Permission of Theaterwissenschaftliche Sammlung University of Cologne/Sammlung Werner Nekes (joint ownership: University of Cologne/DFF/Filmmuseum Potsdam).

> Est mihi huiusmodi machina, quae in ingentem omnes admirationem rapit, dum respicientes loco naturalis faciei nunc lupinam, modo caninam, iam alterius animalis faciem intuentur. (I own a machine of such a kind that enraptures everyone in great admiration, while they receive themselves with the face of a wolf, a dog, or any other animal, instead of their natural face.) (Kircher 1671: 784a)

To our eyes, Kircher's machine looks familiar and antiquated at the same time. Our image-obsessed historical moment at the beginning of the twenty-first century – in which images are ubiquitously available and their manipulation is an easy pastime on every smartphone – can marvel at Kircher's ingenuity while smirking about the technological fussiness. But we should not be misled to merely mirror ourselves in this past period.

I would rather insist on the seeming strangeness of the past moment as a point of departure to explore early modern media ecology. The symptomatic amalgamation of science, technologies, religious differences, anxieties, and overconfidence might irritate us, but this irritation is the Ariadne's thread that leads into the complex and contradictory structures of a media ecology that is partly related to our times and experience but also is categorically different.

The early modern period had a word for these phenomena that was as strange and volatile, as cloudy and dynamic, as the field itself: *thaumaturgia*. The Greek word, later cast out from the system of "orderly" aesthetics, meant the art of making wonder, of causing astonishment, puzzlement, admiration, and sometimes even fear. This very concept shall guide our expedition into early modern media ecology and help highlight the specificities and the cultural function of these phenomena.

From Media History to Media Ecology

The challenge of thaumaturgy as a historical phenomenon is that it evades not only our categories but also our models of writing history. Since thaumaturgy is only partly textual, literary history would miss it; since it lacks some hallmarks of what we conceive of as theatre, theatre history in a narrow sense would describe it only as marginal. Even media history, with its focus on modern mass media, would regard it only as an obscure prehistory. But there are potential approaches that grow from this field of media history and that hold more promise for the study of thaumaturgy: critical media history and media ecology. This section will take each of these in turn, beginning with their shared roots in the broader field of media history.

As a scholarly field, media history came comparatively late to the academy. The models of cultural history that evolved in the humanities at the end of the nineteenth century focused on the concept of achievements and innovation: art and literary history were the blueprint for a historiography that put the ingenious *work of art* at its center. Theatre history and later film history, when they arose, were modeled as sidelines of literary and art history.

For this purpose, performances/productions and films had to be read as equivalents to the text – and the director as author.

Media history, on the other hand, emerged in the 1970s with a distinctly different profile: at its core were mass communication, on the one hand, and popular culture, on the other. The starting conditions for this kind of media history were mass media and its technologies. As Walter Benjamin (2015: 211–44) would say, media history became a history of the age of "mechanical reproduction," although the mechanical would later be supplanted by the electronic and the digital. Thus, media history became an intrinsically *modern history*. Theoreticians like Marshall McLuhan (2009) and Friedrich Kittler (2011) turned this implicit technocentrism into the leading principle of their concept of media history.

Consequently, media history conceived of any form and its technological development predating the nineteenth century as mere prehistory, an evolutionary necessity but a deficient step in the teleological process of the advent of modern media. Such an approach is not only reductive and problematic in its inherent agenda but also reproductive of Eurocentric prejudices and hegemonic claims.[2]

In order to avoid these intrinsic patterns, scholars developed new approaches to media history. Following Michel Foucault's model of cultural history, the concept of *media archaeology* was put forth as a way to abstain from this anachronistic teleology. Archaeology offers a guiding metaphor to cautiously reconstruct the context and reveal the background that led to the emergence of specific media: "Archaeology here means digging into the background reasons why a certain object, statement, discourse or . . . media apparatus or use habit is able to be born and picked up and sustain itself in a cultural situation" (Parikka 2012: 6). Though bound to the discourse of modernity – and with a tendency toward film

---

[2] Friedrich Kittler (2011: 80–1), for example, argues in his influential essay *Optische Medien* (Optical Media) that, because they lacked the mathematical understanding, Chinese artisans simply were not able to produce proper one-point perspectives. This is not only wrong in terms of the underlying facts but also indicative of the cultural bias woven into this historical model (see Kleutghen 2015b).

and photographic representation – the broad field of media archaeology questions the one-dimensionality of media history.

Siegfried Zielinski, one of the towering figures in this discourse, calls for an investigation into the *deep time* of media. The term *deep time*, borrowed from geology, signals a break with the presentist obsession of media history:

> The history of the media is not the product of a predictable and necessary advance from primitive to complex apparatus.... . Media are spaces of action for constructed attempts to connect what is separated.... Instead of looking for obligatory trends, master media, or imperative vanishing points, one should be able to discover individual variations. (Zielinski 2008: 7)

Zielinski's argument points in two directions: first, the refusal of a *grand récit* turns against an evolutionary logic that is so often intrinsic to technology-focused approaches. Focusing attention on the "individual variation," the obsolete technique, and the maverick apparatus allows for a more comprehensive understanding of the underlying cultural processes. But, second, defining media as "spaces of action" invites a perspective that looks beyond that single phenomenon to its broader context. Lisa Gitelman (2006: 7) has therefore emphasized that media history cannot focus on the apparatus alone but must acknowledge that "[media] structures include both technological forms and their associated protocols." She concludes: "If media include what I am calling protocols, they include a vast clutter of normative rules and default conditions, which gather and adhere like a nebulous array around a technological nucleus. Protocols express a huge variety of social, economic, and material relationships."

The interplay of apparatus and protocol became even more visible in the 1980s, when the material residues of these media practices resurfaced prominently in major exhibitions. One protagonist of this development was German filmmaker Werner Nekes (1944–2017), whose interest was originally limited to precinematographic techniques but who eventually compiled one of the world's largest collections of optical devices, including magic lanterns, *cameræ obscuræ*, and peep boxes, along with books and pictures.

Beginning in 1984, he curated and contributed to multiple major exhibitions that had a lasting impact on the field.

Being an artist himself, Nekes did not restrict himself to scholarly writing (his own or others') but rather worked directly with the objects, thus helping surface a marginalized and partly suppressed history.[3] He produced a series of six films on these techniques, titled *Media Magica*, and his major exhibitions were accompanied by massive catalogs that not only presented lavish images of the objects but also categorized them and incorporated the latest scholarship (see, e.g., Dewitz and Nekes 2002; Mannoni, Nekes, and Warner 2004; Nekes and Kienninger 2015). Marina Warner (2004: 15), who cocurated Nekes's 2004 London exhibition, emphasizes the historicity of visuality, even when it seems to be completely private, as in the imagination:

> The veridical or truth-telling status of visual phenomena constitutes an acute puzzle precisely because we cannot think without pictures and these do not always represent objects that exist in the sensory world. In the field of optics, many instruments were created to analyse and reproduce vision. . . . But optics also reflects ideas about consciousness at any given period; it expresses the potential of the inward eye for every generation, the concepts of cognition and mental projection, and the irrepressible tendency of the mind to assemble random marks into intelligible data.

The interplay between imagination, the pictures that form our thinking, and the techniques and technologies that form our social and cultural environment draws attention to the contingency of historical constellations. The "pictures" Warner talks about do not merely mirror the world but create a view of the world, and they define our field of action, feeling, and thinking. In her foundational book *Phantasmagoria* (2006), Warner

---

[3] Writing in performance studies, Dwight Conquergood (2002) emphasizes that the paradigm of textuality is inherently hegemonic.

explicitly points to the stage as an intrinsic part of this circulation and picture-making. With respect to Shakespeare, she states,

> Theatre realizes illusions, setting up a perceptual paradox about the play-world that cannot be resolved. The dramas that seem to resolve the problem of the supernatural, by breaking the spell and destroying, or at least limiting, the powers of ghosts and fairies, are the same plays in which Shakespeare meditates most obsessively on the debatable state of illusion itself and the power of fantasy.... The uncertainty this produces relates to the condition of the theatre itself, oscillating between event with consequences and an utterance or description as airy and ephemeral as the break taken to speak. (Warner 2006: 135)

Warner's description of the ambiguous status of theatre – between being real and being "airy and ephemeral" – resonates with an argument most recently made by Pascale Aebischer. In her much-acclaimed study *Shakespeare, Spectatorship and the Technologies of Performance*, Aebischer (2020: 2, 13) proposes a "historically grounded spatial theory of technologically mediated spectatorship." She critiques the way that the Elizabethan theatre has too long been fashioned as "pure" in contrast to the complex theatrical apparatus of recent centuries: "imagining the early modern stage as a technology-free haven of unmediated communion between performer and audience is a nostalgic fallacy." Doing away with this romanticization of the "empty space" allows for a perspective in which, for example, the spatial arrangements of the Elizabethan stage can be understood as deeply mediating the audience's experience.

From the perspective of theatre/performance historiography, Tracy C. Davis and I (2021: 3) have proposed that theatre and performance history be considered as parts of a larger project of *critical media history*:

> Critical Media History focuses on processes of formatting or trans-formatting the experience of performance and forms of media. Here, "critical" recognises that concepts

constitute and continually build the ways in which an audience spectates and values a genre, style, media form, or other tradition, as well as the factors that inspire anyone to perform (in any capacity and permutation of this concept). This formation of media not only refers to semiotic, aesthetic, or other hermeneutic factors but also explicitly includes legal, social, political, military, economic, technological, and other constitutive conditions. In this sense, Critical Media History cannot be governed by any definition of theatre or performance – notwithstanding how influential and powerful these might be – but arises from the recognition of complex interrelations and interdependencies.

Critical media history is based on the recognition that every definition of theatre – vis-à-vis other forms of art and media – is rooted in certain cultural and aesthetic presuppositions that define boundaries and criteria. The center of gravity of critical media history is not the concept of fixed unities – *the* theatre, *the* cinema, and so forth – but rather the complex interplay of techniques, cultural practices, material conditions, modes of reception, and critical discourses that lead to the formation (and transformation) of cultural categories and models.

Critical media history shares with media archaeology its interest in formative processes, an emphasis on the possibilities of "alternative genealogies for the development of technology over time" (Wynants 2019: 4). However, where media archaeology is vertically oriented (as Zielinski's metaphor of *deep time* suggests), critical media history considers the *Sitz im Leben* (a seat or place in life) of media – that is, its situatedness in the life of a society and especially in a certain historical moment (Davis and Marx 2021: 19).

The *Denkfigur* (figure of thought) of *media ecology* points in a different direction: comprising the tension between natural structures and human-made artifices, the concept (a *contradictio in adjectu*) highlights the contingency of a social and cultural environment and the interdependency of elements of differing natures. Thus, media ecology challenges us to think in pluralities and interrelations instead of in essentialized and homogenizing categories.[4]

Emphasizing connections and intersections on various levels, the concept of media ecology has emerged as "a mode of reasoning that foregrounds the whole in its internal interconnectedness and equilibrium [and] also entails an emphasis on how changes in a single variable alter the configuration of the whole" (Heise 2002: 15). Ingo Berensmeyer (2016: 330) stresses that the concept of media ecology accentuates the idea of spatial networks – a fact we might understand as expanding on Zieliniski's idea of "spaces of action":

> "To take the step from media anthropology to media ecology is to acknowledge the increasing relevance of spatial networks, locations and patterns of mobility in media and cultural studies, as well as the importance of the network concept with its origin in cybernetics and its implications of multi-level interconnectedness."

If critical media history centers processes of locating, historicizing, and scaling in its methodological profile, then media ecology substantiates these processes in various ways and highlights interconnections as well as the relation of performer and apparatus. In this sense, the notion of media ecology makes various claims:

- Ecology highlights a multifactorial web of interrelations across different elements and social strata.
- Ecology focuses on systems but does not assume that these systems are static or equilibrious. Change and transformation, without a clear purpose, are founding conditions.

[4] Boaventura de Sousa Santos (2007: 66) has made this argument of multiplicities with respect to his notion of "ecologies of knowledge": "It is an ecology because it is based on the recognition of the plurality of heterogeneous knowledges (one of them being modern science) and on the sustained and dynamic interconnections between them without compromising their autonomy. The ecology of knowledges is founded on the idea that knowledge is interknowledge."

- Ecological thinking includes a reflection on the material conditions and the various forces (economic, epistemic, social, and juridical) that effect this system.
- Ecological thinking is bound to pluralities and contingencies – different elements exist and develop differently in varying biotopes. But the term also invites a reflection on the interconnectedness and the mutual influence of these various biotopes.
- Media ecology does not hypostatize its contained elements but rather historicizes them and analyzes them in relation to the various biotopes.
- The historiography of media ecology thwarts the Eurocentric or Occidental bias that is so prevalent in technocentric approaches. Its very focus calls for increased attention to connected histories (Subrahmanyam 1997), specifically to the question of how these connections are built and acted on.

What are the consequences of such a concept of media ecology when applied to the early modern period? Whereas our twenty-first-century perspective relies on categories of art and media that have emerged since the age of Enlightenment, the early media ecology is less strictly organized and classified. In this sense, it is genuinely premodern. The historical concept of thaumaturgy – a broad but vague umbrella term – might offer an entrance point to this labyrinthic and highly dynamic field.

Thaumaturgy: Wonder-Making

The Greek term *thaumaturgy* covers a broad field of phenomena in the early modern discourse: from religious wonders to astonishing occurrences (see Bloch 1924). Despite its religious overtones, the concept can be found on all sides of the denominational divide. In his tract on Euclidian mathematics, English astronomer John Dee (1527–1609) gives the following, rather vague, definition: "Thaumaturgick, is that Art Mathematicall, which giveth certaine order to make straunge workes, of the sense to be perceiued, and of men greatly to be wondered at." He complements this definition with a varied yet unsystematic list of examples: a "brasen hed ... which dyd seme to speak"; "As, to see in the Are, a loft, the lyvely Image of an other man, either walking to and fro: or standyng still"; and "For in

Noremberge, A flye of Iern, being let out of the Artificers hand, did (as it were) fly about by the gestes, at the table" (Dee 1570, n.p.).

It is evident that Dee does not try to give a complete list but rather names a few examples out of a plethora of potential references. At first glance, we might stumble over Dee's definition of thaumaturgy as an "Art Mathematicall," yet his reference to mathematics underlined that these wonders were not supernatural but somehow in accordance with the laws of nature. It is precisely the link between mathematics and magic that is at the core of this discourse. Cologne-born magus Heinrich Cornelius Agrippa von Nettesheim (1468–1535), in his influential *De occulta philosophia* (*Three Books of Occult Philosophy*, 1531–3), states that mathematics is indispensable for any magic (Agrippa 1651: 167–8; see also Yates 2002: 150–1).

The question of magic is exactly the abyss above which all discourse about thaumaturgy trembles in the early modern period – not merely as an academic question but also, at least in parts, as a real question of life and death because the Inquisition and other forms of witch hunt were more than real.

Spanish-Flemish Jesuit Martín Del Rio (1551–1608) offers a systematic approach to the problem in his *Disquisitionum magicarum libri sex* (*Investigations into Magic*, 1599–1600). Del Rio was erudite and well read, and his books – though published only in Latin – circulated in more than twenty editions until 1755. He orders the field in three different categories: *magia naturalis*, *magia dæmonica*, and *magia artificiosa* (i.e., natural magic, demonic magic, and artificial magic).

The *magia artificiosa* is based on mathematical principles, as Del Rio (2000: 51–2) points out, offering a list of examples that notably resemble those found in Dee and Agrippa (clearly there was a repertoire of phenomena that occupied the collective imagination):

> Artificial, operative magic is of two kinds, *mathematical* and *deceitful*. I call "mathematical" that magic which rests upon the principles of geometry, arithmetic, or astronomy: for example ... the combustions caused by mirrors during the siege of Syracuse; Archytas's wooden doves which could fly; the Emperor Leo's twittering birds made of gold; ... and many similar things which have been described in history

books. Hero and Pappus call this magic "thaumaturgy." Such magic, however, surely cannot achieve anything which runs contrary to nature since it lacks the power of natural causes and the specific movement and dimensions of these when they have been brought into the equation, as is obvious in the case of Archimedes's mirrors or in modern hydraulics and automata.

Though based on laws of nature, these practices can become evil if they deceive spectators:

The other type of magic is theatrical and deceptive and can, indeed, be called *deceitful* (which is why the wonders done by magicians were called "toys" and "sleights of hand" by the Greeks, and "games," "amusements," and "objects of derision" by the Romans. . . .) To this category belong most of the things people believe jugglers, itinerant performers, and tightrope walkers did by the means of spells (*incantationes*), but which they actually accomplish because of the agility of their feet and hands. (Del Rio 2000: 52)

Here, Del Rio reveals a subliminal, antitheatrical resentment that runs through his argumentation (see, too, Agrippa 1651, Cap. XLVIII). It is not surprising that while he ascribes legitimacy and harmlessness to the *magia artificiosa*, he is still suspicious about those who perform it in public:

Wonder-working magic, like natural magic, is of itself both good and licit, as all arts of themselves are good. Both, however, may become illicit (a) when they produce an evil result; (b) when they give rise to scandal and people think that these things happen through the agency of evil spirits (and in consequence things of this kind should not be permitted unless the entertainers have public and appropriate attestation of their art from Catholics); and (c) if some spiritual or temporal harm to body or soul threatens the entertainer himself or the spectators (for which reason those who, without necessity or just cause, expose themselves to the danger of death through entertainment are damned). (Del Rio 2000: 53)

While the "wonders" are harmless as long as the performer does not make bigger claims (like possessing the force to conjure spirits), any exploitation of the audience's good faith would be illicit. This is because Satan himself exploits laughter and lightheartedness to seduce people to sin and mischievousness: "Satan loves to provoke others to laugh so that while they are laughing and happy they may imbibe impiousness. This tricksters, jugglers, pranksters, comedians, and itinerant entertainers often enchant their very judges who are enticed into absurd joy and astonishment and account everything mere fun and not something which ought to be punished" (Del Rio 2000: 54).

Thaumaturgy in this sense is the art to make people wonder, referring to an effect on the spectators rather than an intrinsic quality of the phenomena themselves. The ambivalence of the sensation of wonder is paradigmatic for the period, although in later writings, as in those by German Jesuit and scientist Gaspar Schott (1608–66), a disciple of Athanasius Kircher, the focus shifts to the proficiency and technical aspects of the presentation of these wonders (see Schott 1677: 16–20).

Gottfried Wilhelm Leibniz (1646–1716), who was not merely an influential German philosopher and polymath (on this term, see Burke 2020) but also an important organizer of scholarly and scientific networks, events, and occasions, envisioned in his *Drôle de Pensée* (*An Odd thought concerning a New Sort of Exhibition*, 1675) a cabinet of objects that were gathered to build a "theatre of nature and of art" (Wiener 1940: 235). The aim of this institution clearly meets the concept of thaumaturgy: "As to the public, it would open people's eyes, stimulate inventions, present beautiful sights, instruct people with an endless number of useful or ingenious novelties" (Wiener 1940: 239). As Horst Bredekamp (2004: 62) has argued, Leibniz's imagined theatre programmatically mixed and mingled various categories to increase knowledge and to stir scientific curiosity. In contrast to his theological counterparts – with whom Leibniz was in close correspondence – he was not afraid of a potential "contagion" by bringing together performers, actors, acrobats, and inventors. To him, they were all parts of a larger continuum. But, at the same time, the very institution of the *Wunderkammer* (cabinet of curiosities) had an apotropaic effect: assembling all these objects, practices, and performers in one place also allowed them to be kept at distance from everyday life (Daston and Park 2012: 255–61). Unlike the wandering performers, who would show up in all sorts of locales, these objects and performers were thus insulated, prevented from broader intermingling.

Philosophically, thaumaturgy remains the unloved changeling of these various spheres. German philosopher Alexander Gottlieb Baumgarten (1714–62), a representative of the early Enlightenment, was the last to attempt to turn the shimmering and ever-evasive term into a solid philosophical concept. His *Aesthetica* (1750), echoing earlier traditions in its Latin prose, defines thaumaturgy as causing curiosity through novelty (see Baumgarten 2018 [1750]: 822). Whereas later aesthetic theories discarded thaumaturgy from their systematic approach because it always seemed to be in danger of mere superficiality, Baumgarten's triangulation of novelty/admiration/curiosity justifies the *æsthetica thaumaturgia* because the raised curiosity fosters an increase in knowledge and reflection. But Baumgarten's own prose testifies against his attempt to define a regular *æsthetica thaumaturgia*. His intricate argument cannot eclipse the delicate balance that has to be struck to meet the right degree of novelty and not create a "mere" spectacle.

The proximity and connection between thaumaturgy and the *magia artificiosa* (and, respectively, the *magia naturalis*) bore serious consequences for the performers/artists engaged in this field. John Dee (1570: n.p.), right after giving his definition of thaumaturgy, complains about common prejudices:

> And for these, and such like marueilous Acted & Festes, Naturally, Mathematically, and Mechanically, wrought and contriued: ought any honest Student, and Modest Christian Philosopher, be counted & called a Coniurer? . . . Shall that man, be (in hugger mugger) condemned, as a Companion of the Helhoundes, and a Caller, and Coniurer of wicked and damned Spirites?

Dee's tirade against those denunciatory accusations of witchcraft was not entirely out of the blue. He himself had repeatedly been under public suspicion – not the least during his days as a student when he designed a flying machine for the staging of Aristophanes's *Peace* (Dee 2013: 5–6). Athanasius Kircher (2011: 12), for his part, remembers a similar episode from his days as a young novice when he designed scenery for a theatrical performance in Heiligenstadt that caused such astonishment among spectators that he was accused of witchcraft. Obviously, no performers – social rank or ecclesiastical status notwithstanding – were exempt from these accusations and suspicions.

It would be reductive to reflect on thaumaturgy merely from an intellectual history perspective. The lens of media ecology rather challenges us to consider the situatedness of wonders while placing them in the larger context of the intellectual climate of the early modern period. In this sense, it is important to acknowledge that this is not an exclusively Occidental history but rather a genuinely "connected history" in the definition of Sanjay Subrahmanyam. These wonders, one can argue, even play a constitutive part insofar as

> ideas of "connected histories" [are] based on the idea that the relations between cultures must be mediated and that this mediation involves among other things the production (rather than the mere fact) of commensurability. Rather than to posit that visual cultures were either commensurable or incommensurable, we need to focus on the acts that produced commensurability. (Subrahmanyam 2012: 209)

Commensurability was constituted not only by joint axioms but also by these wonders, which challenged predominant epistemologies. These connected East and West, as Subrahmanyam (2019: 280) has stated: "we cannot easily separate the knowledge that circulated in the Persianate world of the Mughals, Safavids, and Ottomans from that which flowed through the Iberian world-empire of the Habsburgs." In his attempt to "explore the location of 'wonder,'" he focuses on natural phenomena such as spectacular creatures and monsters (for an expanded case study, see Zadeh: 2023).

As Subrahmanyam (2019: 318) argues, wonders are culturally bound but can be translated and transferred to other cultural contexts – creating the foundational commensurability on which cultural connections can be built.[5]

The Arab language also had a term for the aesthetic pleasure of wonders: *'ajā'ib*. Marina Warner (2011: 6) has argued in regard to the *Arabian Nights* – a text that circulated among European cultures beginning in the early eighteenth century – that the aesthetic category of *'ajā'ib*, "meaning marvels, wonders, astonishing things," is central to the narration (see also Mottahedeh 1997). Indeed, the tales include not only magical beings of all sorts but also human-made technical wonders such as automata and flying machines (see especially the story of the "ebony horse"; Warner 2011: 387–9). The prominence of these apparatuses is significant in two ways. First, it gives proof to Subrahmanyam's thesis that we should look for the circulation and translation of knowledge rather than assume that Western and non-Western epistemologies were categorically different from each other. Wonders – in all the broadness provided by the vague term – might prove to be a prime place for these kinds of circulation.

Second, it suggests that the centrality of wonder in the relation between the European and Persian cosmopolis might not be entirely accidental. While Subrahmanyam (2019: 279) refers to works of natural history from antiquity, such as those of Cicero, Pliny, and Augustine, he leaves out one whose inventions and texts have been a common source for both Europe and the Persian cosmopolis: Greek mathematician and engineer Hero of Alexandria (c. 10–70 CE). But regardless, this circulation of wonders is not limited to the residues of Greco-Roman antiquity; it reaches as far as India, China, and Japan (Flores 2007).

If we abstain from the idea that the early modern period is marked by the "renaissance" of classical antiquity (imagined as being primarily Occidental

[5] Stephen Greenblatt (2017: 14) made a comparable argument by defining *wonder* as the "initial European response to the New World," a definition that highlights the different forms and directions that wonders can take depending on their varying contexts.

and White and traced through an imagined Byzantium; see Liudprand 1915: 488; Daston and Park 2012: 92) and instead try to grasp this period in its enormous volatility, fragility, and excitement, thaumaturgy becomes a central term to denote equally the limitations of epistemological models and the sensational fascination of experiencing these limits as a sphere of potentiality.

Minds, Hands, and Heads

A history of early modern media ecology can be written neither in the oxygen-free realm of pure ideas nor as a chain of technological developments. It calls for a perspective that equally considers the social and cultural context as well as the protagonists who live and work in this field.

Twentieth-century English historian Frances A. Yates was foundational in deconstructing the European perception of the Renaissance as being driven by the "rediscovery" of the antique classics. Neither were these writings "discovered" – they were often circulated through translations from Arabic or Hebrew – nor were these the only circulating ideas and concepts. Historical events such as the conquest of Constantinople by the Ottomans in 1453 or the expulsion of the Jews from the Iberian Peninsula and the start of Christopher Columbus's expedition, both in 1492, mobilized people and communities and intensified an exchange between the three major monotheistic religions around the Mediterranean Sea. In contrast to furthering a genuinely Western *grand récit*, Yates (2001, 11–18) centers Catalan mystic Ramon Llull (1232–1316) and other scholars who represent the interreligious and transcultural climate of the late Middle Ages and the early modern period.

Yates calls her project of locating an alternative philosophical tradition (influenced by the Jewish Kabbalah and esoteric writings and unfolding in the interplay of Judaism, Christendom, and Islam) "occult philosophy," and many of her protagonists, such as John Dee or Heinrich Cornelius Agrippa von Nettesheim, also feature prominently in the history of thaumaturgy. While she focuses almost exclusively on the history of ideas, her choice of words (Latin *occultus*, hidden) emphasizes a hegemonic system that is based on the division of legitimate and illegitimate forms of knowledge.

Boaventura de Sousa Santos (2007: 66) has described this division as the "abyssal line" that organizes the fields of power and control in the system of Western hegemony, and he proposes instead the notion of multiple "ecologies of knowledge." As a way to describe the social condition under which these ecologies develop in the shade of a hegemonic system, he introduced "liberated zones," or "spaces that organize themselves according to principles and rules radically opposed to those that prevail in capitalist, colonialist, and patriarchal societies. Liberated zones are consensual communities, based on the participation of all their members. They are of a performative, prefigurative, and educational nature" (Santos 2018: 31).

The ambivalence that marks such liberated zones – in their continual fluctuation, to meet the needs of their members – is indicative of the social position of early modern media ecology. Performers and actors across Europe and Asia were, for the better part of the early modern period, often legally disenfranchised, sometimes even enslaved, and they appear in our archives only as subjects of control and punishment. Their trade was not considered honorable, and up until the eighteenth century, they were forced to live at the margins of the emerging bourgeois society. While their work was hailed and enjoyed at best, their social and legal status was fragile and under constant threat. Owing to the mobile nature of their work, they were often marginalized as vagabonds, experiencing all the aggression and suspicion connected with migration on so many levels.

Yet to merely project the goals and rules of bourgeois, capitalist societies onto these actors would mean to subject them once more to hegemonic ideology. To understand the historical dynamics surrounding these figures, we must instead get a deeper understanding of the restrictions and discriminations as much as of the liberties and possibilities that their marginalized zones offered. Of course, the challenge is that the abyssal line has rendered them invisible. It is not only that they most often did not speak or write for themselves; in most cases, they are only an absence in our records. Imtiaz Habib offered a groundbreaking response to such questions in his 2008 study *Black Lives in the English Archive, 1500–1677*, in which he called for a new calibration of theory and archival work "so that the facticity of the archives becomes the mandate for theory and the construction of theory writes the reconstructed facts of the English early modern age" (Habib 2008: 11). The very concept of early modern media ecology calls for a comparable approach, reevaluating the lacunæ of existing records and paying attention to the figures who barely make the limelight.

Little do we know, for example, about the unfortunate Jewish performer Baṭrūnī, who – during the reign of Uthmān b. Affān (644–55) – performed a show in the city of Kufa, in present-day Iraq. Terrified by the spectacle of the *illusion* (so the story goes), one spectator drew his saber and killed the performer on the spot, while his audience felt urged to say a prayer against the devil's harm (for this recounting, see Al-Masudi 1865: 264–68 [in Arabic/French]; Moreh 1992: 13–14 [in English]). German scholar Georg Jacob (1925: 46) interpreted the "illusion" as a shadow play. Like many other performers, Baṭrūnī himself is little more than a shadow in the archival records, rather forcing us to guess and speculate about his performance. Yet his cruel death opens two further lines of consideration. The first is as *anecdote*: the fact that Al-Masudi describes him as a Jew hints at the important role that minoritarian communities played in the performance and dissemination of media ecology. The anecdote reveals how their liminal status granted them certain liberties but was at the same time a source of danger.

But the story about Baṭrūnī's fate also represents a certain *scenario*: the presentation of new media triggers shock and (sometimes) violent rejection in an inexperienced audience. Diana Taylor (2003: 28) defines scenarios as "meaning-making paradigms that structure social environments, behaviors, and potential outcomes." This particular scenario can be traced from the Mongol court of Ögedei Khan (Jacob 1925: 11–13) and its reception of Chinese shadow players, through rumors of magic performances by both Albert the Great (Scheeben 1932: 201–3) and Rabbi Loew (Bischoff 1903: 88), and into countless ages, places, and cultural environments. Reading the Baṭrūnī scene not merely as anecdote but also as scenario thus allows us to construct an intercultural network of references (see Cabranes-Grant 2016: 25–31).

But attention also needs to be paid to disenfranchised groups within a cultural context. Bleak is our knowledge about Margaretha Waltherin from Mühlhausen, Germany, who in 1594 applied for a license to present her "Himmelreich" (Kingdom of Heaven) in Nuremberg but did not receive it (Purschke 1981: 225).[6] She is one in a long line of female principals who appear in the records applying for performance licenses, sometimes in their own name, often for male relatives (husbands, fathers, and brothers). Sometimes the patriarchal system is imprinted on them – when they appear, for example, as *Widow le Rouge*, who unsuccessfully applied for a license in Basel (Switzerland) in 1698. Female contributions to the field of media ecology are generally read as symptomatic of social precarity and deficiency rather than as inventive or artistic. Yet their presence is quite well documented (e.g., in administrative files). As a first, superficial survey of performance data in the German-speaking sphere indicates, female entrepreneurship has been steady and constant (Marx 2021b: 153–4). And it offered a kind of female agency and autonomy that were probably more liberal than in the system of guilds, which treated women as patriarchal property.

The concept of media ecology does not only imply an extension of the scope of interest and research or a rewriting of the leading categories. As a concept embedded in the larger discourse about decolonization, media ecology seeks a new approach to the protagonists who shaped and constituted the social sphere in which these media appeared. The following sketches do not claim in any way to achieve comprehensiveness or to emphasize the most important actors. They are rather meant to offer a reflection on possible approaches to media ecology and the challenges they bring about.

Urbi et Orbi: *Kircher, Grimaldi, and the Jesuit Network*

The metamorphosis machine of Athanasius Kircher is one of those apparatuses that still stir the imagination. To this day, Kircher is either hailed as the "last man who knew everything" (Robinson 2006) or derided as a caricature of a failing scientific system. Clearly, in his days, he was

---

[6] The term *Himmelreich* refers to a type of mechanical puppetry that received its name from the depiction of biblical scenes. Unfortunately, no such apparatuses or visual depictions have survived, but there is evidence that they were quite popular in various European countries (Purschke 1979: 27–34).

celebrated as a polymath, although many of his theories proved spectacularly wrong (Burke 2020: 63–4).

But, first and foremost, he is the iconic representative of one of the most elaborate networks in the early modern period, one that stretches from continent to continent and still has a clear center, independent of any dynastic quarrels: the Societas Iesu. Founded in 1540 by Ignatius of Loyola (1491–1556), this new order was significantly different from existing monastic communities and soon became a key element in the Counter-Reformation.

Kircher, born in Geisa, Thuringia, in 1602, entered the Societas Iesu in 1618, the very year that marks the beginning of the Thirty Years' War. After extensive studies in philosophy, theology, and the sciences, he was appointed to teach at the *Collegium Romanum* (Roman College) in 1634. For the rest of his life, Kircher remained at the center of the Catholic world, situated at the core of the Jesuit community as well as the Papal States. Significantly, in 1651, he opened his *Musæum Kircherianum*, one of the most famous *Wunderkammern* of the era (Figure 3; see Mayer-Deutsch 2010).

Kircher did not follow a specific system in his collections but rather tried to argue for a coherent, divine world order that was to be deciphered. Meanwhile, his numerous writings, in their own way as arbitrary yet omnivorous as his selection of objects, were often lavishly illustrated, echoing the sumptuousness of his physical collection. Kircher's concept of scientific work clearly had a strong sense of spectacle and thaumaturgy to it – and both his collection and his books can be understood as prominent instantiations of his thinking. The much-referenced second edition of *Ars Magna Lucis et Umbræ* (1671) exemplifies how Kircher was much less an ingenious inventor than a vociferous compiler whose explanations were meant to testify to his theological convictions.

With respect to early modern media ecology, two lines of investigation help contextualize Kircher's writings and collection vis-à-vis his Jesuit network: the role of imagination in the context of Ignatian spirituality and the global connectedness of the Societas Iesu.

Figure 3 Frontispiece of A. Kircher & G. de Sepibus, Amsterdam, 1678, *Romani Collegii Societatis Jesu Musaeum Celeberrimum*. Permission of Universitätsbibliothek Heidelberg.

The Role of Imagination in the Context of Ignatian Spirituality

The Societas Iesu, approved by Pope Paul III in 1540, is based on the teachings and particularly on the *Spiritual Exercises* (published in 1548) developed by Ignatius of Loyola (see Endean 2017). In their original form – obligatory for every Jesuit – these exercises are arranged in four weeklong stages, together composing a thirty-day silent retreat intended to be not a space of learning but rather a realm for individual experience. Imagination, understood as "an active power, not a passive capacity," is the motor of these practices, which are meant "to form rather than to inform" (Sluhovsky 2017: 75, 71). Meditative techniques should train the individual imagination and teach the discernment of spirits. In contrast to other forms of Christian contemplation, the *Spiritual Exercises* do not aim at facilitating an emphatic experience but rather foster an "indifferent" spectatorship of the imagined scenes to allow for proper judgment (see Shea 2017). In this sense, Ignatius's model echoes, and not accidentally, models of theatrical spectatorship. It is also egalitarian: while the exercises are intrinsic to the formation of every Jesuit, they are not exclusively addressed to the clergy, and they require neither theological training nor any ecclesiastical rank to complete (Sluhovsky 2017: 72).

In stark contrast to the iconoclasm that accompanied the Protestant Reformation, Jesuits fostered imagination not only through these individual exercises but also through renewed imagery: by commissioning and fostering the development of the arts, both sacred art and theatre, so much so that forms of art and media became intrinsic to the Jesuit mission. Kircher's compilation of marvelous objects in his *Musæum Kircherianum*, as well as the compilation of inventions and techniques in his numerous publications, addressed these phenomena in a similar way. While Kircher has often been criticized for not being an inventor in his own right (Lipton 2021: 4–7), he was a gifted presenter and *explainer* (though often wrong in his suppositions). His writings and collection of objects provided a repository from which his Jesuit confreres and other public personæ could draw.

The Global Connectedness of the Societas Iesu

Since the Jesuit order is nonmonastic (i.e., not cloistered in monasteries), Jesuits focused on offering education in Europe and establishing missions abroad. In keeping with Ignatius's praxis of social and cultural immersion, some Jesuit stations consisted of only a small group of priests, who were encouraged to experience the other culture as much as possible from a dialogic perspective. Thus, Jesuit missionaries often became deeply embedded in their host countries and cultures. To compensate for the lack of a formal, external cohesion, the superior of every community was obliged to report regularly to the central Curia in Rome (Fleming 2017). Thus, the order built a unique network providing extensive firsthand information of other cultures that was primarily used for the purposes of the Societas and was partly published (*Jesuit Relations*, 1632–73), establishing the "global interconnectedness of early modernity" (Lehner 2016: 124).

In this respect, the Jesuit encounter with the empires of Asia (Ottoman, Safavid, Mughal, and Chinese) challenged European thinking radically. In particular, China, as a non-Islamic empire, fascinated and puzzled Europeans, their religious denomination or nationality notwithstanding. It is small wonder that one of the first destinations for the Jesuit mission was China, where Italian Jesuit priest Matteo Ricci (1552–1610), who arrived in 1582, established a policy of accommodation and adaptation to Chinese customs and culture (see Standaert 2017a: 160). For our focus, the reign of Kangxi Emperor (born 1654, reigned 1661–1722) is of special interest. In this period, the Jesuits were an integral part of the imperial court and served as astronomers, engineers, and scholars. One leading figure was Flemish Jesuit Ferdinand Verbiest (1623–88), who was head of the astronomy office of the court. He had studied, among other places, at the *Collegium Romanum*, where he was a first-year student in theology in 1651, the year Kircher opened his museum. Although there is no definite evidence of an encounter between the two, it is hard to imagine that Verbiest had no knowledge about Kircher's work and collection. Under Verbiest's guidance, the Jesuit mission became a center for scientific and scholarly advice but also a resource for machines and techniques to entertain the emperor and his entourage (Figure 4; Golvers 2010: 291–3).

Kangxi Emperor's enormous appetite for scientific discoveries but also for sensational machines, music, and the arts opened a pathway for the Jesuits and laid the foundation for a substantial dialogue.[7] One of Verbiest's

---

[7] Catherine Jami (2012) provides a comprehensive discussion of the Jesuit influence on the development of the sciences from the Chinese point of view.

Figure 4 Garden of the Xitang Mission. In: F. Verbiest, Peking, 1668, *Astronomia Europaea sub imperatore Tartaro-Sinico C'am Hyappellato*, n.p. Permission of Bayerische Staatsbibliothek (W 2 P.or. 18).

closest associates in this task was Italian Jesuit Claudio Filippo Grimaldi (1638–1712), who in 1672 presented a "*lucernâ mathemicâ*" (mathematical lantern) to the emperor (Letter JapSin 162). While it is unclear whether this apparatus was actually a *Laterna Magica*, we know for sure that he later produced one in his Beijing workshop (Golvers 2010: 95, 107). Around the same time that Kircher published his compendium of optical devices,

Grimaldi impressed the Chinese emperor with his *magia thaumaturgia*.[8] Even seventy years after the event, French Jesuit historian Jean Baptiste du Halde (1739: 72–3) gave a detailed account:

> The late Emperor Cang hi, whose chief Delight was to acquire Knowledge, was never weary of seeing or hearing them: On the other hand the Jesuites, perceiving how necessary the Protection of this great Prince was to the Progres of the Gospel, omitted nothing that might excite his Curiosity, and satisfy this natural relish for the Sciences. They gave him an insight into Opticks by making him a Present of a Semi-Cylinder of a light kind of Wood; in the middle of its Axis was plac'd a Convex-Glass, which, being turned towards any Object, painted the Image within the Tube to a great nicety. The Emperor was greatly pleased with so unusual a Sight, and desired to have a Machine made in his Garden at Peking, wherein, without been seen himself, he might see every thing that pass'd in the Streets and neighbouring Places. They prepared for this purpose an Object-Glass of much greater Diameter, and made in the thickest Garden Wall a great Window in the Shape of a Pyramid, the Basis of which was towards the Garden, and the Point towards the Street: At the Point they fixed the Glass-Eye over against the Place where there was the greatest Concourse of People; at the Basis was made a large Closet, shut up close on all Sides and very dark. It was there that the Emperor came with his Queens to observe the lively Images of every thing that passed in the Street; and this Sight pleased him extremely, but it charmed the Princesses a great deal more, who could not otherwise

---

[8] In addition to being the subject of the extensive report that I quote from here, this event was remarkably well recorded for its time. It was discussed in the annual letter by the superior (January 12, 1673; Archive of the General Curia JapSin 162) and briefly noted in a work by German writer Johann Christoph Wagner (1688: n.p.).

behold this Spectacle, the Custom of China not allowing
them to go out of the Palace.

The media performance of the apparatus is not unilateral, in the sense of
Grimaldi simply impressing his audience with a foreign object. On the
contrary, it responds to their demands and translates the optical apparatus to
the new cultural environment, even facilitating a method of engagement in
public life for the emperor's concubines, who, owing to the segregationist
gender order of the Confucian society, were prevented from personally
participating.

Like many of his fellow Jesuit missionaries in China, Grimaldi was so
successful that he rose to the rank of mandarin. He gained the emperor's
trust and was appointed imperial envoy (Baldini 2010: 123–64).

From a historiographical point of view, Grimaldi and Kircher – from
their respective positions in the Jesuit network – represent two different
models of authority in their public appearance. Kircher, situated at the heart
of the Societas Iesu and at the Papal court, represents a centrally rooted
model. Stephen Greenblatt (2017: 123) describes such a model:

> There is a type of historical authority that draws its strength
> and coherence from its massive centeredness, its ability to
> situate itself at the institutional and moral core of its parti-
> cular culture. From this stable, well-defended position the
> possessors of such authority pass judgment on what is
> brought before them, and they are suspicious of whatever
> resists the great centrifugal [*sic*] pull toward the center.

Kircher made ample usage of the centripetal logic of the Jesuit network, and
the information to which he had access poured into his numerous publications as well as into the collection of his museum. Intellectually as well as
materially, the world seemed to be at his disposal.

Grimaldi, on the other hand, is a type that Greenblatt (2017: 139)
describes as "the interpreter, the translator, the go-between." Indeed,
Grimaldi not only presented Western techniques and sensations to his
Chinese audience but also provided information about the Chinese court

to his European interlocutors, both within the Societas Iesu and beyond it, as his constant exchange with Gottfried Wilhelm Leibniz proves.

Whereas the position of the centralized authority can be defined as stabilized by textual forms, Grimaldi's authority was based on the performance of his skills as well as of his persona and had an underlying fluidity that also made him a figure of suspicion to both sides. This fluidity is evident in the way he literally changed costumes (dressing again as a mandarin) upon returning to China after a trip to Europe (partly as an imperial envoy, partly as a Jesuit reporting to Rome) in 1694 – and was received with the pomp of the imperial court (Baldini 2010: 167). It is also evident in the fact that Grimaldi never referred to Kircher's book on China (*China Monumentis*, 1667), which was under heavy criticism from contemporaries – be it out of respect for his fellow Jesuit or out of a sense of discipline (Baldini 2010: 136–7). Whereas Kircher's writing increasingly met the skepticism of his fellow scientists in the Western discourse, the in-between position of the Chinese missionaries was brought to an abrupt end through the Chinese Rites controversy (c. 1633–1742) (Standaert 2017b). In the course of this controversy, Pope Clement XI (following an indictment from Dominicans and Franciscans) forbade the Chinese rites practiced by Jesuit missionaries. This ruling infuriated Kangxi Emperor so much that he expelled all missionaries from China (Lehner 2016: 115–16). Thus, the experiment of a genuine cultural, religious, and intellectual encounter was brought to an end in favor of the "purity" of the Western religious system.

Invisibility and Agency: Female Performers and Businesswomen

In contrast to Grimaldi, Kircher, and other protagonists who acted and performed as members/representatives of a larger institution, professional performers were of a precarious social status. The German legal language is particularly blunt, counting them among the *Unehrliche* (insincere) and thus adding a pejorative tone to the social category (Beneke 1863). As Natasha Korda points out in *Labors Lost* (2011), her foundational study on women and the early modern stage, the highly regulated and guild-based early modern European economy created a broad sector of informal economic activities.[9] The involvement of women in this sector crystallizes all its legal, social, and economic ambiguities and contradictions.

The situation varied across England and the continent: whereas some cities allowed women to join guilds or (as in the case of Cologne) to form female guilds, most female entrepreneurship happened in the informal sector, in which media ecology is mostly situated. While England – London, to be more precise – developed a firmly established theatrical scene (and has been the subject of most scholarly discourse on the topic), most of the European theatrical landscape was shaped by wandering troupes. Economically, these troupes were never exclusively performance-focused but usually had some business on the side, trading in goods, medicine, soaps, or some such item. This is particularly true for the Savoyards, who traveled as hawkers and carried their peep boxes and magic lanterns along with small goods of all sorts (Augel 1971).

In contrast to arguments that mobility was only an accidental element for these troupes (Hanser 2020: 11), I view it as essential not only to their social status but also to their economy and cultural impact. With respect to the wood trade in early modern Germany, historian Paul Warde (2006: 284) has suggested differentiating between two models of ecology: "The 'territorial ecology' implies a repeatable set of actions happening at a particular place. It is a process that reinforces the 'integrity' of a particular way of doing things. The 'transformational ecology,' put bluntly, does not. Eventually it must result in the disturbance of local processes; it is a problem generator." Whereas networks established permanent structures that allowed for continuing interaction, the wandering performers were welcomed but also often treated with suspicion. They represent equally cross-pollination and interruption.

The development of a media ecology, and especially the theatrical landscape, was driven by increasing commercialization (Davies 2023: 172). Although the early modern London stage is often thought of as all

---

[9] Korda (2011: 22) explains: "The concept of informality renders visible a wide array of commercial activities occluded by the 'apparently all-pervasive' formal economy, which in early modern England was regulated by both guilds or livery companies and civic officials."

male (based on the identity of most performers),[10] the wider business enterprise of the stage offers a very different view: "Women were active in the early modern theatre industry, particularly in their ownership or management of venues" (Davies 2023: 182; and see 182–94). On the continent, purpose-built theatres were still a rarity, and the infrastructure was less permanent and professional. Here, women contributed to the life and work of the touring companies more prominently. Female performers are documented in Italy as early as 1564, but the practice is probably older and would have spread from there to all over Europe. In the German-speaking sphere, female actors in dramatic performances were first documented in the 1650s (Katritzky 2005; 2008). In other parts of the media ecology, their activities can be traced back well into the sixteenth century. Various female principals applying for a license to present puppetry are found in magisterial records. But, as one might suspect, the archives offer only scattered clues as to their activities, not a comprehensive picture.

An interesting case that allows for some deeper insight is that of Catharina Elisabeth Velten (c. 1646–1712). Although we have no visual or extensive written record of her, we know a little bit about the family she was born into. Her father was Carl Andreas Paulsen (c. 1620–1769), who claimed to be one of the last English Comedians, although he actually might have begun his career in the Dutch troupe of Johann Baptista van Fornenbergh. Paulsen, whose troupe toured extensively in northern Germany and Denmark, is a transitional phenomenon: bridging the gap between the English and Dutch troupes of the sixteenth and early seventeenth centuries and the emerging German troupes (Pies 1970). Catharina Elisabeth grew up in this touring troupe and is believed to have performed from early on.

---

[10] Korda (2011: 18) discusses this assumption critically and concludes, "while the paradigm of the 'all-male stage' had long rendered [women's performance] activities … invisible, scholarship emphasizing female participation in other arenas of theatrical activity has focused almost entirely on detailing the forms of this participation rather than on understanding the gendered division of theatrical labor it has thereby revealed."

In 1671, she married Johannes Velten (1640–92), a runaway from a bourgeois background who even received a magister degree from the University of Leipzig (Heine 1887). Velten succeeded his father-in-law as principal of the troupe in 1676. After his death in 1692, Catharina Elisabeth continued his work as head of the troupe until her death in 1712.

Although we can assume that Catharina Elisabeth had a lifelong commitment to the stage, it is her husband who figures prominently in most historical accounts: Magister Velten (as he is venerably called in older historiographies) is often praised as the "proper" founder of German theatre because he came from a literary-academic background and aimed to introduce the literary drama, especially Molière, to the German stage. Yet what these teleological narratives eclipse is that Velten was far from exclusively focused on literary theatre. Rather, he provided a broad repertory of theatrical wares, performing along with puppets and also with shadow figures. In May 1688, Velten announced a performance of a *Dr. Faustus* play. This event's playbill advertises numerous special effects (flying dragons, fireworks, and so on), ending with "Italiänische Schatten" (Italian shadows) (Tardel 1926: 282). Catharina Elisabeth kept up with this broad variety of performative forms, using them strategically and according to the situation. In 1712, by which time most of her members had left the troupe, she even presented a show of only marionettes in Cologne (Jacob 1938: 13).

The example of the Veltens reveals the permeability of the various spectacular genres but also the restrictive perspective of a traditional theatre historiography: whereas older histories focus on the question of literariness and hail Velten for his academic and learned background, the textual remains of his performances (playbills, supplications, and magistrate decrees) document equally the presence of spectacular scenery, special effects (flight machines and fireworks), and animated figures, be they shadows or puppets. The nomenclature of the documents is blurry but interesting in its evocative character: *docken* but also *polcinella* for puppets, alluding to the *commedia dell'arte*; "Italian shadows" for shadow figures.

Here, we can see the transformative ecology of the touring troupes at work: cross-pollination and competition forced the artists to be versatile. Not only, as Tiffany Stern (2013) has rightly suggested, did performances encompass varying arrangements of human actors and objects (along with scenery and stage machinery, as we can gather from Velten's 1688 *Faustus* playbill), but techniques and skills were constantly mixed and intermingled.

We must not forget that most such decisions were less aesthetic than economic in motivation: given the varying profitability of the different forms, it was an advantage to adjust one's operative profile. While the high costs of a troupe of human actors required a certain minimum number of performances, for puppeteers even a shorter period could be attractive (see Purschke 1980: 37). Versatility helped minimize risk for the enterprise as such.

The example of the Veltens also reveals the (gendered) expectations and norms that fuel classical historiography: while Magister Velten became a hero in the *grand récit* of the emerging bourgeois, dramatic theatre, Catharina Elisabeth was probably much more experienced when it came to the day-to-day business and the practicalities of running a troupe. But bourgeois historiography values formal education over the skills Catharina had acquired by being born into the trade – implementing a gender bias inherent in a patriarchal society.[11]

Something else that can be learned from the case of the Veltens is the social constitution of these practices. The decision to become a performer was a choice not merely of profession but also of social status and way of life. Marginalized by mainstream society, the troupes formed a social cosmos in their own right, in which training and skills ran in the family, and membership was often defined by kinship rather than contract. The Veltens clearly experienced the marginalization that came with this status, and the increasingly fanatic resistance to theatre in the Protestant regions haunted them at various points in their lives. Catharina Elisabeth experienced it in all its cruelty when, in 1675, while she was about to give birth to her daughter, the magistrate of Lübeck forced her husband's troupe out of town – regardless or because of her condition (Hefter 1936: 40). When Johannes Velten fell severely ill in Hamburg in 1692, the clergy of the city refused him the Eucharist as well as the last rites before his death.

---

[11] Claire McManus and Lucy Monro are spearheading research into this area; see their project Engendering the Stage at https://engenderingthestage.humanities.mcmaster.ca/.

The fight against performance culture became a signature activity among ultra-Protestants at the end of the seventeenth century. Echoing Willam Prynne's (1633: 555 v) formula of "the Play-house is the Devils Chapell," pamphleteers attacked performers and players in the most rude and offensive tone. When Magdeburg preacher Johann Joseph Winckler (1670–1722) aggressively turned against Catharina Elisabeth and her troupe, she would not have it. She responded in a widely circulated and reprinted tract titled *Zeugnis der Warheit vor die Schau-Spiele oder Comödien* (Testimony to the Truth of Plays or Comedies, 1701; see Niessen 1940). Here, picking up on the high tone of scriptural references that Winckler had used (from the Bible to John Chrysostom), she defends not only the theatre as such but also female performers like herself. She offers an interesting reinterpretation of the much-quoted passage in Saint Paul's letter to Timothy (1 Tim. 2:12) where he condemns women to silence: "But I suffer not a woman to teach, nor to usurp authority over the man, but to be in silence." Turning the argument around, Catharina Elisabeth argues with some bravado that Saint Paul in other passages emphasizes the equality of women and men and the female authority in all private matters (1 Cor. 7:16; Titus 2:3–5). Thus, she deduces, female actors are not to be condemned simply on principle. She concludes her pamphlet by attacking Winckler for denouncing her and all actors in general despite his own lack of profound experience. She even calls him a slanderer, hinting at the fact that vague concepts such as honor and reputation had a serious juridical and social dimension in her day. For her, this was not a matter of taste, manners, or theological conviction but a question of economic, social, and physical survival.

Given the pamphlet's numerous references and learned voice, it is evident that Catharina Elisabeth Velten had at least some help in meeting her offender eye to eye. We might call this an act of subversive ventriloquism: she borrows (or, rather, lends herself to) a learned voice that meets the registers of her opponent, but it is she who is defending her trade and the work of her life. Her act of standing her ground in the public arena and fighting against fundamentalist hostility was exceptional in her day.

We must not romanticize the conditions of these troupes: their members were cast out from society, largely disenfranchised, and rendered vulnerable to the despotism of authorities on all levels. Santos's (2018: 31) concept of the liberated zones is troubling here in its anachronism, as he coined the term for groups that form deliberately in resistance to existing structures. Yet the criterion of being performative and prefigurative is helpful: the commitment to taking an active part in the media ecology as a performer (of whatever sort) also meant a commitment to creating agency. While the guild system was rigid, the transformative ecology of the theatrical and media landscape offered opportunities for participation and autonomy.

Talented Hands and Minds: Johann Franz Griendel

At last, we come to someone for whom we have a picture: Johann Franz Griendel (1631–87), who is depicted with tools of two of his more noble occupations: the map of a fort and a telescope (Figure 5). Griendel studied at the University of Innsbruck from 1650, entered a Capuchin monastery in 1655, and, upon leaving this monastery in 1670, moved to Nuremberg and opened a workshop for optical devices. Nuremberg was a center of commerce and innovative artisanry and offered the right kind of national and international attention for his new business (see Doppelmayr 1730). In 1677, Griendel moved on to Dresden, where he became a princely engineer. He left for the imperial court in Vienna in 1684 and died there in 1687.

Griendel's biography invites various readings and offers rich material to trace several developments, among them the denominational clash and the emergence of a new class of bourgeois experts. Here, I focus primarily on the Nuremberg episode of his life. Among the cities in the German-speaking realm, Nuremberg has always held a special place because it was as much a center for commerce as it was for the Protestant movement. In the early modern period, it also was a center of the arts, closely linked to playwrights like Hans Sachs (1494–1576) and Jakob Ayrer (1544–1605) along with painters like Albrecht Dürer (1471–1528).[12]

---

[12] The cities of the Netherlands also provided the perfect climate for the flourishing of this mixture of science, artisanship, and exchange on various levels, as exemplified in the Musschebroek family and its workshop (see Wagenaar, Wagenaar-Fischer, and Duller 2014: 27–53).

PR.ÆNOBILIS AC DOCTISSIMVS DN₀ IOANNES FRAN=
CISCVS GRIENDL DE ACH ET WANKHAVSEN.ᾳ.
MATHEMATICVS OPTICVS ET INGENIEVR.ᾳ.

Figure 5 Portrait of Johann Franz Griendel. Permission of Herzog August
Bibliothek, Wolfenbüttel.

For Griendel (1685: n.p.), this biotope allowed him to start a new life and
excel in his new business, as is recorded in a rare document with a list of his
products: telescopes, microscopes, cameræ obscuræ, and two kinds of magic
lanterns. Of these two, one was useful for presenting portraits, hunting
scenes, and "entire comedy of all kinds of things," and the other was
intended to project images "at night across the street on the wall of
a house or in a darkened room . . . as to believe that it were sheer magic;
these find particular usage in occupied forts."

While the connection between the magic lantern and questions of fortification foreshadows Griendel's later occupation, the references to *comedy* and *magic* indicate to what extent Griendel also excelled in performing the techniques he manufactured and sold. As German mathematician Johann Gabriel Doppelmayr (1688–1750) noted, many (national and international) travelers stopped to see his "Curiosa optica" (Doppelmayr 1730: 111). French traveler Charles Patin (1633–93) gives a full account of such a performance:

> M. *Grundler*, a Monk, who (as he saies) had lately embrac'd the Reform'd Religion, according to the Doctrine of *Luther*. But to justifie to me the change of his opinion it wou'd be requisite for him to have as much command over Men's Reason, as he has over their Eyes, to which he represents whatever he thinks fit, and in any manner whatever at his pleasure; for he is absolutely Master of the most abstruse Secrets in Opticks. This is that Art (My Lord) which is capable of fixing half the World in a Point, and which has found out means to extract visual Repercussions out of Chrystal, and to draw near the most remote Objects by certain Reproductions of *Species* and Correspondences of Prospects, which are extended in the most limited spaces from the Distances as far as the Eye can reach. In short, 'tis that fallacious Art that deceives our Sight, and which with the Rule and Compass disorders all our Sences. But our Artist proceeds yet farther; for he can even remove Ghosts from their Stations at his pleasure, without any assistance from the Infernal Regions. Some mention has been already made to Your Most Serene Highness of that Sphœrical Looking-glass, which receives the several *Species* of remote Objects thro' a small Thread of light, and which rolling about in the dark, imprints 'em on it, and causes 'em to follow its Motion; so that real Phantoms and Ghosts are now no longer sensible of the other World. I know divers Persons of great courage who have chang'd pale at the sight of these Sports and of these Magical Artifices.

And with M. *Grundler*'s good leave, all the Esteem that I had of his profound Learning, was not able to free me from the Dread which seiz'd upon my Spirits on that occasion; insomuch that I was apt to believe that there never was in the World a greater Magitian than he: For it seem'd to me as if I had a sight of Paradise, of Hell and of wand'ring Spirits and Phantoms, so that altho' I know myself to be endu'd with some measure of Resoluteness, yet at that time I wou'd willingly have given one half to save the other: All these Apparitions suddenly disappear'd and gave place to Shows of another Nature: For in a moment, I saw the Air fill'd with all sorts of Birds, almost after the same manner as they are usually painted round about *Orpheus*, and in the twinkling of an Eye, a Country-Wedding appear'd to my view, with so natural and lively a representation that I imagin'd myself to be one of the Guests at the Solmenity. Afterward the *Horizon* of my sight was taken up with a Palace so stately, that nothing like it can be produc'd, but in the Imagination; before which there were divers Personages running at the Ring: These Heroes seem'd to be the Gods that were ador'd by Antiquity, and among them 'twas pleasant to observe *Momus* mounted upon a *Barbary*-Horse; and making Satyrical Reflections upon *Jupiter*, who had made a false step amidst so jolly a company. But let us put an end to these Visions and endeavour to divert Your Most Serene Highness with somewhat that is more solid. (Patin 1696: 233–6)

Patin's report resonates with the full range of thaumaturgy, including aesthetic sensation, the fascination with and uncanniness of the magic realm, and an appreciation for scientific and mechanical skills. The description is one of the few full accounts of a lantern show, highlighting not only the aesthetic effect but also the dramaturgy of the "entire comedy of all kinds of things." It is symptomatic of the collective imagination of the early modern period that Griendel's show includes Christian iconography (paradise and hell) as well as the gods of antiquity. Obviously, the show mobilizes and presents the entire European *Denkraum* of the period.

Although Griendel's optical devices were quite unusual, Doppelmayr (1730: 314) – in a catalog of the professions and arts of Nuremberg – indicates that Griendel was embedded in the city's broader artisanal landscape, which included the workshop of Abraham Helmhack (1654–1724), a glassmaker who also produced painted lantern slides.

A totally different yet comparably spectacular trade was that of the various mechanical artisans who produced impressive automata, among them Johann (1591–1670) and Gottfried (1634–1703) Hautsch, father and son. Both built massive panoramas depicting biblical scenes, various workshops, or military scenes (Doppelmayr 1730: 300–1, 304–5). These automata – echoing the earlier practice of the *Himmelreich* – were sold to the major courts in Europe, including the Danish, the French, and the imperial court in Vienna. Skills and knowledge circulated among these families, sometimes guilds, but the accumulation of highly specialized mechanical and optical artisans preconditioned the emergence of a transformational ecology that attracted visitors and spectators and also prompted orders and recommendations from far away. Jessica Keating (2018) has traced six small, clockwork automata and their travels across the Holy Roman Empire, the Ottoman Empire, and the Mughal Empire from the German town of Augsburg.

Techniques and Apparatuses: Material Traces

Media ecology puts an emphasis on the material dimension of media history. But the apparatus is not only a discursive phenomenon (something that is talked about); it is something that must be *read* and integrated into the historical analysis. Thus, the following sketches present some apparatuses and the historiographical challenges connected with them.

Scena

The collective imagination of early modern theatre is often overshadowed by the predominant presence of the Elizabethan theatre, particularly Shakespeare's Globe, not only in the sense of its dramatic legacy but also through what we perceive as the visual record of its material structure. Although this visual record is skewed, the Globe and its late twentieth-century revenant have created a sense of an actor-centered theatre that well suits our modern/postmodern expectations. As Pascal Aebischer (2020: 3–4) rightly points out, the coalescence of the historical record (and its alleged absence of any scenography) with Peter Brook's (1968) postulate of the "empty space" as a "bare stage" has created the idea of the Elizabethan theatre as "purely" dramatic and performative, without the "distraction" of visuals or machinery.

This contemporary projection also eclipses the semantic vagueness that surrounded the field of theatre, media, and performance. William N. West (2021: 2–15) argues that the semantic field of *play* was wide and ambiguous. Callan Davies (2023: 4) comes to a similar conclusion concerning the *playhouse*, refuting the idea of an archetypal form and stressing instead a multiplicity of forms and constellations: "'Playhouse' was an elastic term, which covered numerous architectural forms and types of venue. They were specifically designed or adapted for commercial play, with some degree of regularity. Playhouses were almost always multifunctional, hosting a range of activity that fell, in early modern English, under the remit of 'play.'"

Playhouses had a deep influence on their urban surroundings. For West (2021: 144, 146), they were even considered to be "a likeness of thinking": "Playhouses think. . . . Playhouses did not think like persons; . . . Playhouses think through persons. They think in the sense that they collect, disperse, impose, and transform behaviors." This centrality in the formation of a collective imagination turns the playhouse itself into an object of visual fascination. Yet the semantic field of *theatrum* was as broad as it was vague. Comparing depictions of *theatra* in early modern prints, such as the Straßburg Terence editions of 1493 and 1496, makes it quite evident that the artists associated the place with the activity of looking. But obviously, their images barely relate to a performative or media practice (see Marx 2019: 12–16).

Even a hundred years later, when the magistrate of Antwerp created a sumptuous entry for the Archduke Ernst of Austria, this tradition is manifested. For his 1594 arrival, city artisans designed a massive amphitheatre called a *theatrum pacis* (theatre of peace), in which the auditorium was filled with allegorical figures, representing crafts and social institutions as well as regions and cities (Figure 6). Here, *theatrum* is a symbol of the commonwealth in the broadest sense of the word but is not really a place for performance.

Even a seemingly clear category such as *purpose-built* is not really helpful in the early modern context (Brockett and Hildy 2003: 138). Apart from cities like London and Paris, where a professional, commercial theatre was established, most early modern cities had no need for a permanent, single-purpose edifice. In Nuremberg, for example, performances of all sorts took place at the *Fechthaus* (Fencing House), built in 1627/27 (Figure 7; Paul 2011: 40–59). A convertible, multipurpose venue was much more economical and useful for

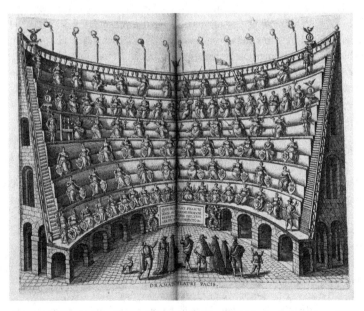

Figure 6 *Theatrum pacis*. In: *Descriptio Publicæ Gratulationis*, Antwerp, 1595, p. 86f. Permission of Theaterwissenschaftliche Sammlung/University of Cologne.

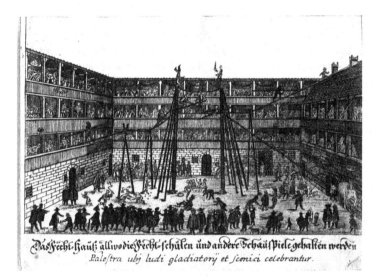

Das Fecht-Hauß allwo die Fecht-schulen und andere Schauspiele gehalten werden
Palestra ubj ludi gladiatorij et scenici celebrantur.

Figure 7 P. Troschel: Fencing house in Nuremberg, 1652. Permission of Theaterwissenschaftliche Sammlung/University of Cologne.

these municipalities than a "proper" theatre. Its convertibility for various purposes also guaranteed control over the performances for the magistrate but without running the risk of having a costly structure unused.

Permanence might have a very different meaning for playhouses than for other cultural institutions (Davies 2023: 9). While Western history tends to favor stone over other materials as an indicator of cultural importance, this might be heavily misleading with regard to venues for something as volatile and dynamic as media ecology. It is well known, for example, that the Globe owes its existence in Bankside (along the bank of the River Thames) to the fact that it was a wooden construction that could be moved from an earlier place in 1599 (Egan 2016: 91–2). As spectacular as this anecdote is, other examples can be found: in 1767, Viennese impresario and Harlequin performer Josef von Kurtz (1717–84) moved his playhouse, including machinery, boxes, and balcony, from Frankfurt to Cologne (Jacob 1938: 58–64).

Venues for other forms of media were even more temporary and volatile: often apparatuses like the peep box were presented in taverns or markets and sometimes even on the streets. There is some visual record that depicts them literally side by side with strolling troupes (Figure 8).

The question of the playhouse concerns not merely the place of performance but also the constitution of the *scena*, the field of vision. To counter Brook's discourse of the idealistic "bare stage," Aebischer (2020: 2) calls for a "historically grounded spatial theory of technologically mediated spectatorship." Robert Weimann's (1978) *locus* and *platea*, as well as the notion of

Figure 8 Depiction of strolling troupes. C. N. Cochin filius: *Foire de Campagne*, 1750. Permission of Theaterwissenschaftliche Sammlung University of Cologne/Sammlung Werner Nekes (joint ownership: University of Cologne/DFF/Filmmuseum Potsdam).

the *discovery space*, serve as her primal references: whereas *locus* describes the fictious place where the plot is set, *platea* (literally the place in front of the medieval scenes where the spectators would stand but also characters would appear) designates a liminal zone of mingling between the theatrical fiction and the reality of the spectators, inviting a kind of performativity that bridges the two spheres.

In continental Europe, the forms were even more nuanced and complex. Following the example of the *Rederijkers*, a Dutch form of performing guilds, the stages for royal entries grew into poly-scenic spatial arrangements that called for a complex and multifaceted literacy on the part of spectators (Figure 9). The arches of these stages offered a variety of tableaux vivants, created by actors, as well as paintings, sculptures, and inscriptions. Additional effects achieved through lighting the scenes are also documented. Stijn Bussels (2012: 12) has emphasized the performative nature of these scenæ: "The performative nature of the entry was further strengthened by the splendid tableaux vivants and triumphal arches erected as decorative structures along the entryroute introducing a complex figurative programme regarding the city and its rulers."

Clearly, these scenæ think in different grammars at one time, and they call for and train a versatility among the spectators. Of course, the translation into print is an additional, important step in this process. What appears at first sight to be a contradictory, at times even confusing, plethora that renders the notion of playhouse/scena/*theatrum* semantically almost empty, is not due to a lack of intellectual rigor or precision; rather, it is symptomatic of the liveliness of early modern media ecology.

Peep Boxes

Carrying wooden boxes on their back and calling for attention, the wandering Savoyards are often depicted with a fundamental device of early modern visual culture: the peep box, also known as the *boîte optique* (French), *rare kiek* (Dutch), or *Guckkasten* (German). Based on the idea of linear perspective, the peep box is a tool to look at printed material through a combination of lens and mirror that intensify the effect of spatial depth (Figure 10).

Figure 9 Scaffold for the royal entry to Antwerp, 1594. In: *Descriptio Publicæ Gratulationis*, Antwerp, 1595, p. 111. Permission of Theaterwissenschaftliche Sammlung/University of Cologne.

Figure 10 Trapeze peep box (c. 1730). Permission of Theaterwissenschaftliche Sammlung University of Cologne/Sammlung Werner Nekes (joint ownership: University of Cologne/DFF/Filmmuseum Potsdam)/Photo Hermann & Clärchen Baus.

The most common pattern of peep-box construction involves an outer case of robust wood that is sized to allow for transportability, a "head" that consists of a large lens, and an internal mirror that reflects the image of a printed sheet put at the bottom. What is interesting in this construction is that the lens does not allow for an Olympian, all-comprehensive perspective – as is usually intended with linear perspectives – but instead magnifies details and becomes blurry at the edges (Figure 11). Thus, in order to see all the details, the spectators have to move their head around, creating some movement in the reception of the image.

The position of the peep box in early modern media ecology was at the intersection of various techniques and trades, most notably lens cutting and printing. Although lens cutting was a specialty of Italian lens makers in the beginning, the skill spread with the course of time. The printed sheets, for their

Figure 11 Detail: lens of the peep box (c. 1730). Permission of Theaterwissenschaftliche Sammlung University of Cologne/Sammlung Werner Nekes (joint ownership: University of Cologne/DFF/Filmmuseum Potsdam)/Photo Hermann & Clärchen Baus.

part, were produced by workshops throughout Europe. Georg Füsslin and colleagues (1995: 26–8) estimate that more than 4,500 different sheets were printed in London, Paris, Augsburg, and Bassano.[13] Peep-box culture flourished in the eighteenth century, fueled by the increase in printing images in general. Most sheets "piggyback" on the expanding visual culture of the time, recycling *vedute* (cityscapes), mythical motifs (like the Colossus of Rhodes), images of catastrophes (earthquakes, volcanos, etc.), or court scenes. Their spectacularity clearly echoes the baroque stage and its machinery as much as

[13] The nomenclature for the sheet varies throughout Europe: *optical view* (English), *vue d'optique* (French), *veduta otticha/veduta prospettiche* (Italian), *opticaprent* (Dutch), and *Guckkastenblatt* (German) (Füsslin et al. 1995: 24). In China, where the peep box was introduced in the seventeenth century, the first written proof is a poem published in 1697, in which the term *Xiyang jingzhi* (Western scenery) clearly referred to the Western origin of the technique (Kleutghen 2015: 763–7).

the expanding interest in technological progress or the encounter with foreign cultures. The peep-box performers, usually wandering persons with more than one trade, could create their own program, using the same box for various sheets. Thanks to its mobility in spatial and social terms, the peep box can be seen as a catalyst of the growing collective imagination.

As for its special effects, the peep box often worked not along the vertical axis but horizontally. Thus, the box could be complemented with various flaps that regulated the amount of light added to the image (Figure 12). If the sheet was accordingly prepared through perforation and the use of motley, transparent paper, effects of illumination could be added, allowing the performer to, for example, simulate changes in daylight (Figure 13a–13c).

A variation of the peep box is the *Perspektivtheater* (perspective theatre) developed and promoted by Augsburg engraver and publisher Martin

Figure 12 Scene of a peep-box presentation. Oil painting attributed to François Rousseau; Schloss Wahn. Permission of Theaterwissenschaftliche Sammlung/University of Cologne.

Engelbrecht (1684–1756). In order to vary the portfolio of his publishing house, Engelbrecht started producing sheets for clipping: consumers could buy the sheets, color them, and arrange the layers in a peep box (Figure 14) (Kleutghen 2015: 84f.). This combination of clipped paper sheets and peep box was certainly inspired by the copper engravings of stage designs that floated through the eighteenth century, facilitating popular printings of works by scenographers like Lodovico Ottavio Burnacini (1636–1707) and Giuseppe Galli Bibiena (1696–1757). Engelbrecht himself produced a series of engravings of the designs of Pietro Righini (1683–1742) (Milano 2016: 14).

The perspective theatre was a modification of the peep box in which the image was presented not on one level but on various successive levels (Figure 15). Thus, the effect of linear perspective is intensified but also modified: gazing through the combination of lens and mirror, the eye is repeatedly caught by various details and forced to continually refocus. The image becomes animated in the sense that its various layers each become a point of attention, the simultaneity of the image thus translated into a succession of foci. It is no coincidence that the subjects of these images resonate with the sense of spectacle that fueled the baroque stage: catastrophes, battles, tempests, and shipwrecks, next to court scenes and exotic spectacles. As Alberto Milano (2016: 11) points out, these peep boxes mark the transition from public exhibition at fairs and pubs to private showings in bourgeois and aristocratic homes.

Over the course of time, *peep box* became an umbrella term for any kind of "little boxes containing something to be seen" (Wagenaar, Wagenaar-Fischer, and Duller 2014: 85). Apart from the boxes that presented printed images, others contained small scenes with little figures. In 1640, the Jesuit school in Cologne designed a *Catoptrix* (lit. mirror maker) to celebrate the centenary of the Societas Iesu (Figure 16). This peep box combined mirrors, lenses, and small scenes (Figure 17a–17d). The four sections presented essential scenes in the life of the Jesuit community: the confirmation of the Jesuits by Pope Paul III, an academic teaching scene, a celebration of Mass, and a martyrdom. This precious apparatus, highly decorated with symbolic characters, offered a glimpse into the life of the Societas Iesu and the various facets of its mission: service to the pope, the Eucharist, science and education, and martyrdom.

Although the peep box is deeply rooted in the European visual technologies of the early modern period, it also quickly traveled beyond Europe, becoming

(a)

(b)

Figure 13(a–c) Peep-box sheet: Piazza di San Marco (Venice); semi-transparent engraving by G. B. Probst (c. 1720). Permission of Theaterwissenschaftliche Sammlung University of Cologne/Sammlung Werner Nekes (joint ownership: University of Cologne/DFF/Filmmuseum Potsdam)/Photo Hermann & Clärchen Baus.

(c)

Figure 13(a–c) (cont.)

one of the apparatuses presented to Kangxi Emperor by the Jesuits. From there, as Kristina Kleutghen (2015b: 769) points out, it was quickly adapted: "Chinese optical views consistently employ the same sort of single-point perspective with exaggerated architectural orthogonals and other depth cues as their European counterparts." Although in the beginning, the peep box circulated only in the narrow circles of the Chinese imperial court and elites, over the course of time it became an intrinsic part of Chinese visual culture: "The geographic and cultural mobility of the European peepbox and its optical views within China thus also acquired social connotations as the device evolved from a rare foreign curiosity in the seventeenth century to a fully sinicized, widespread popular entertainment by the late nineteenth century" (Kleutghen 2015b: 775).

The Great Art of Light and Shadow

It is not accidental that Athanasius Kircher called his book *Ars Magna Lucis et Umbræ* (*The Great Art of Light and Shadow*), a title that clearly goes beyond the question of media techniques to offer more general insights. While we associate

Figure 14 Perspective theatre with six layers by Martin Engelbrecht (c. 1750). Permission of Theaterwissenschaftliche Sammlung University of Cologne/Sammlung Werner Nekes (joint ownership: University of Cologne/DFF/Filmmuseum Potsdam)/Photo Hermann & Clärchen Baus.

Figure 15 Detail: Lens of the Engelbrechtian perspective theatre. Permission of Theaterwissenschaftliche Sammlung University of Cologne/Sammlung Werner Nekes (joint ownership: University of Cologne/DFF/Filmmuseum Potsdam)/Photo Hermann & Clärchen Baus.

early modern performance with daylight and – important on all potential levels – with the concept of "shared light" (Graves 2009: 534), the interplay of light and darkness was essential to the sensual experience of the early modern era.

People of the twenty-first century barely have a chance to experience darkness and its "terrors of the night" (Nashe 1594), but in the early modern period, darkness was not only metaphorically threatening. Craig Koslofsky (2011: 2–3) proposes what he terms *nocturnalization*, "defined as the ongoing expansion of the legitimate social and symbolic uses of the night," as a hallmark of the early modern period: "Through nocturnalization early modern men and women found new paths to the Divine, created baroque opera and theater, formed a new kind of public sphere, and challenged the existence of an 'Invisible World' of nocturnal ghosts and witches." The interplay of light and shadow,

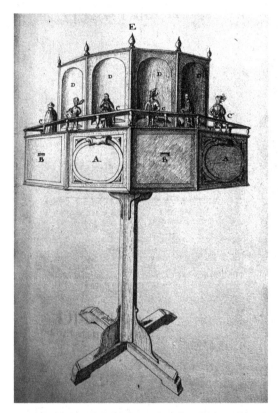

Figure 16 Catoptrix, designed for the Jesuit College in Cologne, 1640. Permission of Historisches Archiv der Stadt Köln, HAStK Best. 150 (Universität) A 1061 fol 324.

including various forms and techniques and also different scenæ in which this difference was acted out, is thus a central axis in early modern media ecology.[14]

---

[14] Avner Wishnitzer has offered a comparable study on the night in the Ottoman Empire; see Wishnitzer 2021.

(a)

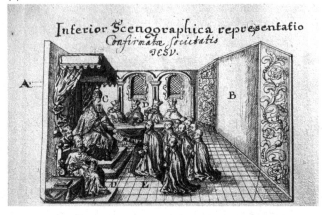

Figure 17a. Scene for the Catoptrix, designed for the Jesuit College in Cologne, 1640: Ignatius receives the official recognition of the order by Pope Paul III. Permission of Historisches Archiv der Stadt Köln, HAStK Best. 150 (Universität) A 1061, fol. 318r.

If we follow the European trajectory, however, it is evident that the Occident came rather late to the party: performances of shadow plays are recorded at about the same time that the first evidence of the magic lantern appears (Jacob 1925: 159–67). In fact, the lack of clear terminology creates an uncertainty that is symptomatic of the general wonder that accompanied the play of light and shadow. For example, although we know little more about the event itself, an entry in the 1677 files of the magistrate of Leipzig is much referenced: "Abraham Werner von Dreßden umb präsentierte er durch eine Magische Latern den Italienischen Schatten auff der Grimmisch" (Abraham Werner from Dresden presents a magic lantern and his Italian shadows on the Grimmisch) (Rudin 2004: 199). In fact, this record conflates two very different forms: the *Laterna Magica* and the Italian shadows, or shadow play. The meager note fuels guesses and wishful projections: we cannot know whether the otherwise obscure Werner was a lanternist or a shadow play performer. And this confusion is not unique to the European context: Ottoman traveler Evliya Çelebi

(b)

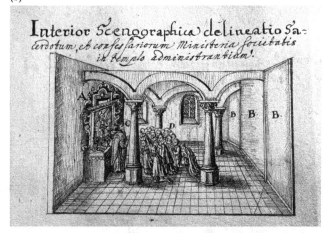

Figure 17b. Scene for the Catoptrix, designed for the Jesuit College in Cologne, 1640: Celebrating mass. Permission of Historisches Archiv der Stadt Köln, HAStK Best. 150 (Universität) A 1061, fol. 319.

(1611–84) also refers to both sorts of performers, those with shadow figures and those with the magic lantern, while the precise distinction remains unclear (Çelebi 1846: 1.2.229).

As dissatisfying as it is, given our modern longing for clear categories, any attempt to solidify these historical terms seems to be more or less futile. But this "confusion" might indicate that these various forms are not distinct phenomena after all but related points in a larger continuum of practices that explored the interrelation (and evocations) of light and darkness. For early moderns, the sensation of encountering the ethereal, luminous apparitions was probably too striking to care about the technological specificities.

As E. H. Gombrich (1995: 17–19) has written, shadows are far from the universal phenomenon that their ubiquitous presence might suggest: in fact, they bear contingent, culturally significant meaning. Thus, it is small wonder that the origin of shadow plays often lies in mythical tales of encounters with the afterlife. There is the legend of the Chinese emperor Wu of Han (156–87 BCE), who asked the magician Shao Ong to conjure up

(c)

Figure 17c. Scene for the Catoptrix, designed for the Jesuit College in Cologne, 1640: Scene of Teaching. Permission of Historisches Archiv der Stadt Köln, HAStK Best. 150 (Universität) A 1061, fol. 318r.

his late concubine (Needham 1962: 122), or the various myths surrounding the Ottoman Karagöz: one legend attributes the form to the remorse of Sultan Orhan (1281–1362), who had called for the execution of two bawdy craftsmen, Karagöz and Haçivat; and another attributes it to Sultan Selim I (1470–1520), who relished in his victory over the Mamluks in 1517 (And 1963: 34). Shadows – real in their appearance yet mysteriously ethereal and simmaterial – were an ideal object of imagination, fascination, desire, and abhorrence.

The shadow play as a performative mode is also the perfect example of a migrating art form: although scholars debate whether it originated in India or in China, it traveled from both countries to the East as much as to the West. Anecdotal evidence indicates the presence of Chinese players at the court of Ögedei Khan (1186–1241) (Jacob 1925: 11) as well as in 1171

(d)

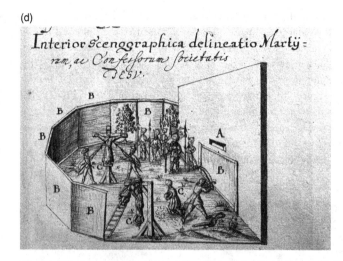

Figure 17d. Scene for the Catoptrix, designed for the Jesuit College in Cologne, 1640: Scenes of Martyrdom. Permission of Historisches Archiv der Stadt Köln, HAStK Best. 150 (Universität) A 1061 fol. 319.

in the city of Mosul, present-day Iraq, from which the practice seems to have spread throughout the Islamic world (Guo 2012: 9). As a performative form in its own right, it reached Europe rather late, and the first reports of shadow performances do not appear until the seventeenth century. In *Della Christiana Moderatione del Theatro* (On the Christian Taming of Theatre, 1655), a diatribe against theatre, Jesuit Giovanni Domenico Ottonelli (1583–1670) mentions "bienti ombranti" (vagrants making shadows); for the German-speaking sphere, the first shadow plays are documented in 1683 (qtd. in Savarese 2010: 164). Clearly, the context of these discussions speaks to an existing practice, not a fresh invention. But the European sources also highlight the migratory nature of the form known as "ombre Italienne" (Italian shadows) or, later, "ombre Chinoise" (Chinese shadows), the nomenclature emphasizing the cultural importation (Jacob 1925: 170–4).

Notwithstanding this belated documentation of shadow plays, moving shadows had caught the European imagination from the time of antiquity, most famously in Plato's Allegory of the Cave. But shadows also had an impressive theatrical life. Samuel van Hoogstraten (1627–78), for example, mentions having directed a "schaduwendans" (shadow dance) (Figure 18; Hoogstraten 1678: 259; Brusati 2021: 291–2). He describes the scene as follows: "When the curtains were drawn, a large audience saw a dance of horned fauns and field nymphs – or, better said, their shadows on the illuminated screen – happily welcoming, so it seemed, the young Acis and the pitch-black Galatea, while Cupid floated

Figure 18 Shadow dance. In: S. van Hoogstraten, Rotterdam, 1678, *Inleyding tot de Hooge Schoole der Schilderkonst*, p. 260. Permission of Niedersächsische Staats- und Universitätsbibliothek Georg-August-Universität Göttingen, HSD: 4 BIBL UFF 69 (6).

in the air, performing all sorts of antics to amuse the party" (qtd. in Brusati 2021: 292).

While Hoogstraten cites his arrangement as an illustrative example for painters, the scene of mythical creatures from Greek mythology and later the *Odyssey* clearly depends on the fluidity of the shadows, which allows him to play with proportions, flying demigods, and more. But Hoogstraten is not unique in this staging of shadows. While systematic research on the subject is still a desideratum, scattered hints clearly indicate the usage of shadows as a theatrical means, as in the Jesuit play *Excitatio Lazari* (Awakening of Lazarus, 1650): "Scena II. Lazarus wird begraben / wirdt alles durch Vmbras repræsentiert. Cum Choro. Scena III. Todtenmahl wirdt auch auff vorige weiß für die Augen gestellt" (Scene 2. Lazarus is buried, all presented through Shadows [Vmbras]. With Chorus. Scene 3. Totenmahl, presented in the same manner).

It is unlikely that these representations were projections as some scholars have assumed (Scheitler 2017: 35–7), because neither artificial light nor lenses were strong enough to produce an image that would have allowed for such an effect in a full playhouse. It is more likely that these *Vmbras* were – as in Hoogstraten's image – cast against some kind of screen by regular actors with the help of a light source.

The announcement of "Italian shadows" as we find it in German playbills after 1683 indicates a different device: an opaque figure casting a sharp silhouette on a screen (Figure 19). The popularity of the theatrical usage of shadows in the seventeenth century is indexed by the fact that German-Latin lexicographer Kaspar von Stieler (1632–1707) created an entry for *comœdia umbratica* ("Lust- sive Spielschatten" [fun- or play-shadow]) in his dictionary (Stieler 1691: 1739). We know little about the performance of these figures, but the few surviving playbills reveal that they were usually sideshows, an additional element in the motley fabric of early modern performances. The first full-time performer of shadow plays as their own form of entertainment was François Dominique Séraphin (1747–1800), who called them "ombre Chinoise" and put them in a different category (Guignollet and Séraphin 1871).

The magic lantern itself makes its appearance in the seventeenth century – relying on a deepened understanding of optics as much as on an improved technique of lens cutting. Although Athanasius Kircher was

Figure 19 Shadow figure: *ombre Italienne* (c. 1800). Permission of Theaterwissenschaftliche Sammlung/University of Cologne.

the first to publish a detailed image of the magic lantern, doing so in the 1671 edition of his *Ars Magna Lucis et Umbræ*, he was certainly not the inventor of the apparatus. Danish mathematician Thomas Walgenstein (1622–1701) and Dutch scientist Christiaan Huygens (1629–95) are equally credited with the invention (Mannoni 2000: 28–58).

An early precursor to the magic lantern is described in a fifteenth-century manuscript of engineer Giovanni da Fontana (c. 1395–c. 1455) (see Fontana 2014). His manuscript includes a sketch and a brief description of a small lantern projecting the image of a larger devil in front of the lantern-carrying person (Figure 20). The Latin description reads: "*Apparentia nocturna ad terrorem videntium*" (Nocturnal apparition to horrify the onlookers). Willem Tebra (1982: 11) has rightly pointed out that this lantern probably could cast only a small projection because "he used it in a room for a private performance." The framing as a "private performance" notably corresponds with Kircher's (1671: 769) much later description of a magic lantern show: "Nos in Collegio nostro in obscuro cubiculo, 4. novissima summo intuentium stupore exhibere solemus" (In our college, we usually show the four last things [death, judgment, heaven, hell] in a darkened room to the greatest stupor of the onlookers) (Figure 21). Two elements are strikingly similar here: the subject of the projection (devils, demons, souls in purgatory, and the "last things") and the rather intimate constellation of onlookers to the projection.

Although Kircher (1671: 769) also mentions that Walgenstein had sold so many lanterns as to make them almost vulgar in nature, the magic lantern was certainly not a mass medium; it was only for small-scale performances. The combination of the subject and the private framing earned the apparatus its nickname "Lantern of Fear." Prototypical here is a performance of Walgenstein's described by Danish naturalist Oliger Jacobaeus (1650–1701). Walgenstein presented the lantern to Danish King Frederick III (1609–70):

> With his lantern, he [Walgenstein] showed various things to the divine Frederick III of Copenhagen, among which must not be forgotten the figure of death, represented to the king some days before his demise. This figure inspired some horror among those surrounding the king, but the king alone, after reprimanding their cowardice, said that above all this spectacle did not appear terrible to him, but joyful, to such an extent that he could not see enough of it. He desired that it should be presented three times, at certain intervals. (qtd. in Mannoni 2000: 59)

The scene points in two directions: on the one hand, Frederick III is shown to perform an exemplary, stoic attitude toward death, fashioning him as a baroque prince; on the other hand, the intimacy of the performance allows

Figure 20 Giovanni da Fontana: Sketch of an early projection lantern. In: G. da Fontana, Venice, c. 1420–30, *Bellicorum Instrumentorum liber cum figuris.* Permission of Bayerische Staatsbibliothek München, Cod. icon 242, 70r.

the images to appeal to the inner images of the spectators. It is not coincidental that the magic lantern as an apparatus not only is situated at the intersection of scientific experiment, technological advancement, and

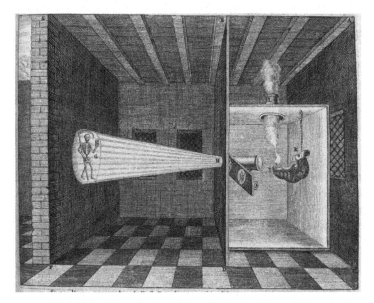

Figure 21 Magic lantern. In: A. Kircher, 2nd ed., 1671, *Ars Magna Lucis et Umbræ*, p. 769. Permission of Theaterwissenschaftliche Sammlung University of Cologne/Sammlung Werner Nekes (joint ownership: University of Cologne/DFF/Filmmuseum Potsdam).

sheer entertainment but also occupies the space of religious, denominational uncertainty. Depicting demons and devils, Death, and suffering souls in purgatory, the flickering scena of the magic lantern allowed for a sensual, spectacular experience of what was unspeakable.

The emergence of the Enlightenment did not stop but rather further fueled this process: the eighteenth century saw the proliferation and metamorphosis of these performances in the séances of necromancers and occultists, culminating in the legendary phantasmagoria performances of Robertson (Étienne-Gaspard Robert, 1763–1837) (Warner 2006: 147–56).

Shadow plays and magic lantern projections offered the sensation of imma-
terial apparitions, fluid bodies, and shifting figures that were seemingly not
bound to physical laws. These "airy nothings" invited multiple and sometimes
contradictory interpretations and, at the same time, defied all conceptual fixa-
tion. Through sensation and spectacle, they explored the limits of light and
darkness, providing a sensual field for the volatile and instable *Denkraum* of the
period.

The Magic of Gunpowder: Fireworks and Mock Battles

In 1582, Sultan Murad III (1546–95) invited the "world" to a celebration,
unparalleled in his day, to mark the circumcision of his son Mehmed. There
can be no doubt that Murad was determined to use this opportunity to
display the richness and cultural superiority of his empire to friends and
enemies alike. For more than fifty days, the Constantinople Hippodrome,
a place designed in antiquity for this kind of mass spectacle, played host to
an excessive display of guilds and military craftsmanship but also of lavish
delicacies and a sensual overabundance (see Terzioğlu 1995).

This festival marks the peak of Ottoman court culture, and its signifi-
cance as a spectacular summit of the most important political powers in
Europe and Asia cannot be overestimated. Among the various spectacles,
a recurring phenomenon was that of fireworks, displayed in various forms
and scenes. In this genuinely transitory form, military mastership, alchemy,
and physics were as much at play as was a sense of dramaturgy and
spectacle. One protagonist of this spectacle was an Englishman called
Edward Webbe (b. 1553/4).

Webbe's biographical account, published in 1590, reflects the major
political and cultural tensions of his day: following his father's example,
he became a gunner and served in various armies. After fighting at the battle
of Tunis in 1573, he was captured by the Turks and became a galley slave.
Facing the miserable conditions ("want of victualles"; Arber 1868: 20),
Webbe identified himself as an experienced gunner and was immediately
drafted into the sultan's army to fight against Persia. After the war ended,
Webbe found himself imprisoned again, but he was relieved from his
confinement to participate in the aforementioned festivities:

Whilst I was remaining prisoner in Turkey, and kept in such
slauish manner as is Rehearsed the great Turke had his
sonne circumcised, at which time there was great tryumphes
and free liberty proclaimed for a hundred dates space, that
any Nobleman, gentleman, traueller, Christian or other,
might freely (without being molested) come and see the
tryumphes there vsed, which were woonderful: I my selfe
was there constrained to make a cunning peece of fire work
framed in form like to ye Arke of Noy, beeing 24 yardes
high, and eight yardes broad, wherein was placed 40 men
drawen on 6 wheeles, yet no man seene, but seemed to goe
alone, as though it were onely drawen by two Fiery
Dragons, in which shew or Arke there was thirteene thousand seuerall peeces of fire worke. (Arber 1868: 28–9)

Memory of the festivities survived the spectacular moment through diplo-
matic dispatches and commissioned reports (Terzioğlu 1995: 97n2) but also
through an impressive series of Ottoman miniatures that provide a rich
visual record. While Webbe's "Arke of Noy" is not depicted, we see other
forms of architecture that were displayed: castles and dragons, wheels and
rockets. These performances as well as their representation in miniatures
soon became a pattern, as the examples from Surname-i Vehbi (1720) show
(Figures 22 and 23).

In these performances, the military character of the fireworks displays
is pretty obvious: the castles were often part of mock battles and pre-
sentations of military skills. Mock battles and comparable forms can be
found in China, India, and the Ottoman Empire as well as throughout
Europe (Needham 1985; Khan 1996; Werret 2010: 18–19; Malayail 2016).
At the English court, water pageantries, which included fireworks, were
particularly popular. These often cited the political situation, as in the
mock sea battle of merchants against Turkish pirates (Chambers 2009:
1.138–9). The theatre of war found a delicate echo in this genre.

The execution of fireworks was the task of specialists who doubled as
entertainers and as artillerists. Gunners were not part of the regular
troupes but were highly trained specialists who either were commissioned

Figure 22 Miniature by Abdülcelil Levni: Fireworks depicted in the Surname-i Vehbi, c. 1720. Permission of Topkapi Palace Museum Istanbul, A.3593 (Surname-i Vehbi, by Levni) fol. 33b–34a and fol. 52b–53a.

for a military campaign or were enslaved like Webbe. Like firearms, fireworks spread from China to the Christian and Islamic worlds. Thus, they were a genuinely intercultural phenomenon; many of the ingredients, first and most prominently saltpeter, were traded from India and Arabia, leaving Europe completely dependent on these imports. The expertise in casting guns, on the other hand, was often imported from Europe (Ágoston 2005: 14–15, 42–8, 96–7). In some German cities, fireworking constituted a guild in its own right, demanding formal training and public displays as exams (Figure 24). But the expertise also ran through other networks. For example, for Leibniz (2006: 11, 18), the aforementioned Claudio Filippo Grimaldi was a much-sought-after informant when it

Figure 23 Miniature by Abdülcelil Levni: Fireworks depicted in the Surname-i Vehbi, c. 1720. Permission of Topkapi Palace Museum, Istanbul, A.3593 (Surname-i Vehbi, by Levni) fol. 33b–34a and fol. 52b–53a.

came to Chinese fireworks, but at the same time Grimaldi designed cannons for Kangxi Emperor according to the latest European standards, which he had probably acquired during a short stay in Poland (Baldini 2010: 157–9). Of course, this circulation of knowledge was perceived with precaution and even fear: as eager as Leibniz (2006: 26–7) was to learn more about China, he was just as anxious that the Jesuit missionaries would give away too much Occidental knowledge and thus create an asymmetry. He admonished the Jesuit P. Laureati to make sure that not only the Chinese profited from this exchange.

The amalgamation of expense, secret knowledge, and extreme force of the explosives marked the early modern fireworks as a demonstration of power:

Figure 24 Scheme for a trial firework by Georg Carl Hornung, Nuremberg, 1665. Permission of Theaterwissenschaftliche Sammlung/University of Cologne.

Fireworks were "secrets," open to certain audiences but not to others, designed to cultivate "the admiration of such as know not the secrecie," or so, at least, the nobility imagined. Gunners labored to provide such artifices.... Such views explain the appeal of pyrotechnics to natural magic, which also dealt in secrets and claimed to be a form of lawful or "natural" enchantment. Magical epistemology hinged exactly on carefully managed access to secret techniques, mobilized to raise the admiration of the vulgar to the advantage of the knowledgeable. (Werret 2010: 54)

In this light, it is obvious that the fireworks display is not merely a spectacular sensation but also a powerful "performance of waste" (Roach 1996: 41 and see 123–4): an excessive mobilization of capital, knowledge, and strength, displayed (and thereby destroyed) without any lasting effect but for the mere joy, terror, and awe of the momentous wonder. Sumptuous miniature castles, fiery dragons, or merely sparkling lights, fireworks were made for conspicuous consumption, expressing knowledge, wealth, power, and force. The English envoy to the Sublime Porte gave Queen Elizabeth a full description of Murad's 1582 display:

Some of the other castles were burnt, which succeeded better; and some models of men on horseback, but full of fireworks, were thrust in among the people, and the rockets and other fireworks with which they were fitted took their way through them. Then a great tent was seen to appear in the middle of the square, all made of fire joined together in such wise that the shape was perfectly kept. This gave much pleasure to the eye, and after lasting a quarter of an hour, suddenly all went out. (Butler 1909: entry for July 21, 1582)

Similar structures are known from European fireworks, such as in the Nuremberg carnival, where artificial castles were drawn in pageants and eventually went up in flames (Figure 25; Roller 1965: 100). The diabolical overtones that mark these structures in the Nuremberg carnival can also be found in the depiction of hell in mystery plays, as Philip Butterworth (2022: 217–70) has pointed out: flames meant light and heat but also indicated the devil's costume.

The sensation of fireworks was too tempting to not bring them onstage and integrate them into the scenic apparatus: volcanos, battles, storms, and thunderstorms were a constant stage presence from the sixteenth century onward (see Jones 2016). Yet fireworks and pyrotechnics were not only a metaphorical but a real danger, threatening the theatre in its material existence. The Globe burned down after a cannon shot on June 29, 1613, but it is only the most prominent case (Chambers 2009: 2.419). Early modern theatre history is full of accidents and casualties. During a passion play performance in Tangermünde, Germany, in 1647, rockets hit the hellmouth,

Figure 25 Artificial castle for a carnival pageant in Nuremberg, illuminated Schembart manuscript. Permission of Theaterwissenschaftliche Sammlung/ University of Cologne.

which started burning; in 1662, Philip IV of Spain was almost killed during a fireworks display (Ernst 1697: 95, 98). The list goes on.

To what extent fireworks and pyrotechnics occupied the collective imagination can be seen from the engravings that try to document these events: the dynamics and explosiveness bring the medium of print to its limits. In this sense, one can wonder the degree to which the danger of these performances was a calculated risk intended as part of the aesthetic pleasure. The engraving of the *ignes triumphales* (triumphal fires) installed for Ernst's entry to Antwerp in 1594 relishes the magnificence but also the danger of the flames (Figure 26). Many of the fire baskets are installed in such a way as to suggest that the houses themselves were burning (*"ut omnia urbis tecta conflagare viderentur"* [as if all the roofs of the town were burning]; Bochius 1595: 131). The textual commentary details the precautions taken and proclaims the luck that no one tripped or fell and that the burning city did not become reality. The relief of the merely virtual catastrophe – also a kind of catharsis – is clearly expressed in picture and text.

Fireworks and pyrotechnics are more than just another facet of what Koslofsky (2011) describes as nocturnalization: they are a lavish luxury to enlighten the night but also conjure the danger, violence, and lethal reality of fire and turn it into a palatable sensation. Imported to the stage, they cite this ambivalence but threaten to transgress the boundaries of play and fiction.

The danger of fireworks – as well as the fascination with their sensation – inspired performers to seek alternatives. So-called artificial fireworks (French *feux pyriques* and German *Chinesisches Feuerwerk*) offered a faint echo of the glittering nighttime displays but were contained in wooden cabinets (Nekes and Kieninger 2015: 459; Wagenaar, Wagenaar-Fischer, and Duller 2014: 80–4). One such display, from Basel at the end of the eighteenth century (Figure 27), projects the image of a flying wizard, echoing not just fireworks displays but a sense of the uncanny fear once linked to this figure. Evoking sensation while only referencing the fear that was "real" one generation earlier, the small apparatus has turned fireworks and witchcraft into a form of "home entertainment."

Figure 26 Fireworks for the royal entry of Archduke Ernst in Antwerp in 1594. In: *Descriptio Publicæ Gratulationis*, Antwerp, 1595, p. 132f. Permission of Theaterwissenschaftliche Sammlung/University of Cologne.

Little is known about the performance practices attached to artificial fireworks. The proximity to peep boxes invites the speculation that these boxes might also have been shown at fairs and in taverns. There is, for example, a 1797 Nuremberg playbill for puppeteer Georg Geißelbrecht (1762–1826), who also performed shadow plays, announcing a "physical firework" and praising it as being without "any smell or smoke" (Eversberg 1988: 110). At the end of the eighteenth century, the genre of "mechanical theatre" emerged, featuring various apparatuses, partly as a pantomimic presentation. Yet the artificial firework marks the transition from the early modern public sphere to the bourgeois salon, the epitome of the new formation of the public sphere in the nineteenth century.

Figure 27 Peep box for artificial fireworks with a flying wizard projected on the small screen (c. 1790). Permission of Theaterwissenschaftliche Sammlung University of Cologne/Sammlung Werner Nekes (joint ownership: University of Cologne/DFF/Filmmuseum Potsdam)/Photo Hermann & Clärchen Baus.

Puppets, Automata, and Other Wonders

The world of the early modern period was not only one of theology, politics, and trade but also one of "spirits, good and bad, fairies, demons, witches, ghosts, conjurors" (Yates 2001: 87). Amid all the early modern tensions of multiple theological discourses, the emergence of the modern sciences, and still-extant cultural habits and practices, the imagination in the East and the West was particularly haunted by the phantasma of soulless matter, animated (from Latin *anima*, soul) and turned into a moving, acting entity. This specter of machines, automata, puppets, and comparable objects is what makes them part of early modern media ecology. The dual forces of fascination/ obsession and anxiety/terror at work here are perhaps best articulated in a thirteenth-century medieval legend. As the story goes, Albert the Great created the first artificial man. When his disciple Thomas Aquinas (1225–74), unaccompanied, came into Albert's office and encountered the speaking sculpture, he was so horrified that he destroyed it. When Albert learned about this, he allegedly yelled at Thomas: "What have you done! Your ignorance destroyed a good deal of my life's work" (Scheeben 1932: 206–7). Albert's robot represents a phenomenon that can also be found in the legend of Rabbi Loew's Golem and in the *Arabian Nights*.

The various trajectories of these phenomena find a crossing point in the person and writings of Hero of Alexandria (c. 60 CE), who not only invented many machines and automata but whose apparatuses had a long afterlife at the Byzantine court.

Automata mark a point of commensurability across cultural traditions in Subrahmanyam's (2012: 209) understanding – but also a point of disjuncture between East and West, as E. R. Truitt (2015: 2) has argued:

> The long history of medieval automata demonstrates also that the turn toward mechanism – to using mechanical models to explain and understand the body, the universe, and the laws that govern both – which is usually taken as one of the hallmarks of modernity of seventeenth-century natural philosophy, stretches back to antiquity. Thinking with automata persisted throughout the Byzantine regions and the Islamicate world through late antiquity and the medieval period. Yet in the Latin Christian West, mechanistic thinking largely disappeared as a way of knowing until the turn of the fourteenth century.

The Reformation and its iconoclasm opened a new and critical debate about medieval religious practices that involved images and statues (Vanhaelen 2022: 84), some of which had movable parts or were physically acted on, like a statue of Christ that "ascended" to heaven.[15] In England, the controversy

---

[15] German art historian Johannes Tripps (2000) refers to such objects as "handelnde Bildwerke" (acting images).

of the Rood of Grace at Boxley Abbey in Kent can be seen as exemplary. The figure on this crucifix could move his head, bleed, and turn his eyes and seemed to respond physically to pilgrims (Butterworth 2005: 123–7). For the Protestant activists who destroyed the figure in 1538, this was proof of fraud by the congregation. Although this figure was clearly embedded in a liturgical or paraliturgical context, it marks the transition to puppetry.

Puppetry was as common in the early modern period as the terms are manifold through which it is described and the techniques used to perform it (Purschke 1979). But the polyphony of forms and terms makes sources hard to interpret. We know, for example, that in 1573 Italian players applied to the Lord Mayor of London for permission "to make shewe of an instrument of strainge motiones," but we do not know what sort of show it was or what kind of "instrument" was meant (Chambers 2009: 4.271).

To further approach this field, a conceptual detour is helpful. Frank Proschan (1983: 4) introduced the concept of *performing objects* as an umbrella term for puppets, masks, and other such items. He writes: "Performing objects ... are *material images of humans, animals, or spirits that are created, displayed, or manipulated in narrative or dramatic performance.* While puppetry is at the center of this definition, it is not alone" (original emphasis). Proschan's programmatically open definition avoids both iconicity and dramatic context. Stephen Kaplin (1999: 32) followed up on this approach by introducing the categories of *distance* and *ratio* to describe the performing object further:

> By "distance" I mean the level of separation and contact between the performer and the object being manipulated – beginning at the point of absolute contact (where performer and object are one) and running through psychic, body, remote, and temporal degrees of contact. "Ratio" refers to the number of performing objects in comparison to the numbers of performers.

Although neither Kaplin nor Proschan had early modern performing objects in mind, their distinctions allow for important clarifications. Many early documents of puppetry in the European context indicate some sort of entire scenery, be it the aforementioned "instrument of strainge motiones," the *Himmelreich* or *Spielwerk* (toy mechanism) of German-speaking performers, or the "Chaos of the World" referenced in a 1623 English license (Butterworth 2005: 134). Although we do not have any surviving apparatus, a few visual records survive.

A broadsheet from around 1700 depicts an itinerant puppeteer carrying a puppetry box on his back (Figure 28). On closer inspection, we can see

Figure 28 Wandering puppeteer with the puppetry box on his back, broadsheet (c. 1700). Permission of Germanisches Nationalmuseum Nürnberg, Graphische Sammlung, Inventar-Nr. HB 23792d, Kapsel-Nr. 1295a.

O Rare Show

Figure 29 Scene of a rare kiek performance; J. Smith after a painting by H. Kerk (c. 1650–1700). Permission of Theaterwissenschaftliche Sammlung University of Cologne/Sammlung Werner Nekes (joint ownership: University of Cologne/DFF/Filmmuseum Potsdam).

Figure 30 Scene of a *Bänkelsang* performance. Oil painting attributed to François Rousseau; Schloss Wahn. Permission of Theaterwissenschaftliche Sammlung/University of Cologne.

that the little scene is populated by devils and a harlequin. From the picture, it is evident that the ratio of figures to puppeteer precludes personification of a single figure by the performer. Clearly, he instead used the puppets to offer narrative framing in his performance.

This distant relation of performer to performing object can also be found in some instances of peep boxes. In one image, the *rare kiek* consists of small scenes, depicted and explained by the performer (Figure 29). This mode is probably the same one in which dollhouses were presented/performed (Korda 2021). A variation on this kind of performance is the *Bänkelsang* (moritat/cantastoria), which was particularly popular in Germany and the Netherlands and in which the performer paired a sung or narrated story with a series of images (Figure 30). Clearly, the concept of performance did

Figure 31 Scene of a peep-box performance; sketch by J. A. de Peters (c. 18th century). Permission of Wallraf-Richartz-Museum & Fondation Corboud, Graphische Sammlung Inv.-Nr. Z 511.

not rely on the idea of personification but allowed for a broader range of aesthetic forms.

Kaplin (1999: 33) adds an interesting observation about technology: "As the physical distance between the performer and the object widens, the amount of technology needed to bridge the gap increases." Some peep boxes included mechanisms that would allow figures to move (Figure 31). A sketch by Johann Anton de Peters (1725–95) offers a rare glimpse into this situation: on one end of the box, we see a person working the machine while the performer-narrator, costumed in a turban, interacts with the audience. His stretched finger on the closed lid of the box might be read as a gesture to emphasize the performative distance of what is seen and what is to be heard.

A small distance, in Kaplin's model, indicates immediate identification, whereas any increasing distance requires more technology. In this sense, automata, self-moving figures and objects, mark the extreme end of this continuum. In the early modern period, they became a luxury and a spectacle in their own right. These automata circulated widely; fabricated in cities like Augsburg, they soon became a commodity widely sought after by courts all around the globe. Thus, these automata exemplify a transformational ecology as they could never hope to find a local market/environment but were always conceived of as circulating across borders. It is symptomatic that many of these objects imitate movement, whether as carts or ships.

Dramatic Echoes: The Drama of Early Modern Media Ecology

How does the history of early modern media ecology relate to the rich and powerful tradition of drama and literary theatre? While for a long time, theatre history was considered a mere subset of literary history, the focus on early modern media ecology emphasizes the differences between the fields and calls for a reevaluation of drama and its interrelation to media/theatrical practices. Recent scholarship has extensively discussed the instability of early modern play texts. Stephen Orgel (2002: 42) made the argument explicit when he stated: "The text was a script, and it was only where the play started; the play, and its evolution into the texts that have come down to us, was a collaboration between author and actors, with the author by no means the controlling figure in the collaboration."

Orgel's diagnosis of the unstable text resonates with deconstructionist theories and with ideas about the *postdramatic theatre* as Hans-Thies Lehmann (2006) defines it. This analogy is meant not to claim an anachronistic relation but to use Lehmann's concept as an analytical device to complicate the interrelation of text and performance.[16] The early modern theatre was not as uniform and clear-cut by literary formulæ as poetological discourses want to believe, and media and theatrical practice was not as clearly dominated by the literary form of drama as Lehmann claims. In light of media ecology, it is obvious that the literary form of drama is the product of a complex formative process that is fueled partly by poetological principles and partly by neighboring media and arts.

The Complex Formative Process at Work

The formation of the literary concept of drama as a piece of literature that precedes the theatrical performance can be described in two different perspectives: on the one hand, by relating early modern play texts to the physical spaces in which they were performed. Situating the texts in a specific physical and social environment also forces us to consider the interplay with other performance practices. A second perspective would look more closely at the interplay of text and performance and question the material conditions of transmitting the texts.

Stage Spaces and Intertheatricality

Robert Weimann, following his foundational *Shakespeare and the Popular Tradition in the Theater* (1978), described two different modes of representation that he identified with the two scenic places in the medieval mysteries: *locus*, the fictional place within the plot, and *platea*, the common ground of players and spectators that allowed for a more physical style of acting, fueled by the immediate communication of players and audience.

---

[16] William Worthen (2014: 7) notes that Lehmann's paradigm is less suited for a historical periodization than for analytical work.

The Elizabethan stage, heir to this preceding scenic tradition, comprehends these two modes. But it also renders the relationship of text to performance superfluous:

> Shakespeare's stage was spacious enough to comprehend, but also to qualify both these traditions. The altogether unequal degree of qualification in either of these modes of performance meant that, intriguingly, boundaries between the verbal signs of language and the visible signs of the body became as porous as they were contingent. For Shakespeare, therefore, the familiar opposition of "performance versus text" (or vice versa) would be entirely unhelpful. (Weimann and Bruster 2008: 9)

Indeed, the poly-scenic structure of the early modern scenæ can be understood as a physical manifestation of the spaciousness that Robert Weimann and Douglas Bruster describe here. An example from Cologne might illustrate the material dimension of this spaciousness quite well: in November 1627, the newly erected church Maria Himmelfahrt, center of the Jesuit College in Cologne, was opened with a *Stephanus* play (Figure 32). For this performance, a tripartite stage was built that allowed for three different scenes: two consecutive segments of the main stage, separated by curtains, and an additional platform above. If one compares the physical structure of the stage with the scenario of the performance – the dramatic text itself has not survived – it becomes evident that these three spaces were not unified under the auspices of a "realistic" space but instead allowed for different levels; the inner part of the central stage was reserved for the center of royal or papal power, and the outer part was dedicated to the other scenes. The upper stage was designated as a celestial level in which Mary and angels would appear. Clearly, the complex cosmological worldview that fueled the play required a spatial expression – an expression that appears as comic to us when, in act 4, scene 2, for example, Stephanus in his oratory is elevated in the air, literally halfway between the mundane and the celestial sphere. As Carl Niessen (1919: 41–2) shows, the tripartite spatial arrangement was an adaptation from the English Comedians. This stage arrangement not only is useful anecdotally to prove the circulation of

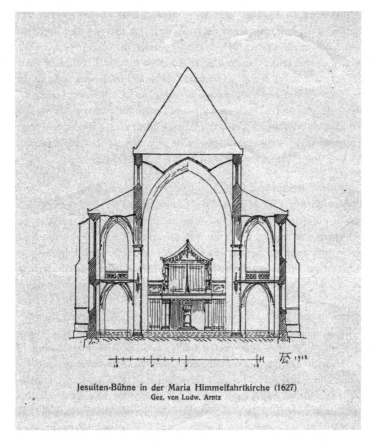

Jesuiten-Bühne in der Maria Himmelfahrtkirche (1627)
Gez. von Ludw. Arntz

Figure 32 L. Arntz: Sketch of the stage for a performance of a *Stephanus* play
by the Jesuit College in Cologne, 1627. Permission of Theaterwissenschaftliche
Sammlung/University of Cologne.

techniques across all national and denominational categories but also draws
attention to the fact that the meaning of such a special arrangement could be
easily adapted to various contexts.

The example also hints at a more general facet of interrelation: the relation of a performance not only to a text but also to other theatrical forms. William N. West (2013: 154) has specified the concept of *intertheatricality* in this sense: "Instead of reading the historical record of early modern theatricality as a collection of allusions and references, it opens the possibility of understanding theatre as made out of other performances." West's definition of "theatre as made out of other performances" is the link to the interplay of media ecology. Thus, we might ask: to what extent were performances not only embellished or illustrated by media apparatuses but also built from them, carrying these forms in their DNA?

Reciprocal Relationships and Theatregrams

William Worthen has addressed the relationship of text and performance from a different point of view. Whereas literary scholars consider the performance as secondary to the text, Worthen (2003: 23) describes the relationship between the two as an interplay of independent elements: "A stage performance is not determined by the internal 'meanings' of the text, but is a site where the text is put into production, gains meaning in a different mode of production through the labor of its agents and the regimes of performance they use to refashion it as performance material."

In the light of media ecology, this reciprocal relationship is interesting in this sense of "put[ting] into production" because it allows for a reading of the text with regard to not only the depiction of character and plot but also certain effects and visual patterns (Worthen 2010: 82). Rebecca Schneider (2011: 89–90) has called for a revised perspective by defining the performance as the record of the preceding text: "In the dramatic theatre, the live is a troubling trace of a precedent text and so … comes afterward, even arguably remains afterward, as a *record* of the text *set in play*" (original emphasis). Pushing this argument even further and connecting it with the idea of intertheatricality, we might ask for a reading of play texts that is sensitive to the resonances of media ecologies and thaumaturgy and looks for their echoes and imprints.

Seeking to transcend conventional categories such as *motif* or *influence*, Louise George Clubb (1989) introduced the concept of *theatregram* in her work on Shakespeare and the Italian theatre. Richard Andrews (2014: 42) defines it as follows: "A 'theatregram' is a unit in a stage plot, or a typical relationship between stereotyped characters, which can be removed from one dramatic context and inserted into another." This concept has been picked up to describe circulation and cultural mobility of early modern drama, especially by scholars affiliated with Theatre without Borders.[17] Theatregrams allow us to speak about the "likelihood of material transmission from one culture to another" (Henke 2014: 31), whether as ideas, figures, or scenarios but always also as a commodity to be traded (Lezra 2014: 201).

While the concept of theatregram leans heavily on the idea of literature and textual elements, from critical media history's point of view it also provides a point of focus on the circulation of effects, apparatuses, and sensations. Gina Bloom (2018: 7) has expanded on this point in comparing plays to games: "If early modern plays are games, then we have to read them differently, studying them in much the way we might other games from the past."

Following this introduction of these two facets of early modern theatre, the next sections turn to examples from the early modern stage and illustrates how the analytical approach changes if the reading is grounded in media ecology.

Magic and Wonder as a Topic of the Stage

Magic and wonder are staples in the performance of the early modern period, most famously in Shakespeare's *The Tempest* (1611), in which magic not merely is mentioned but is at the core of the play. The play's structure differs significantly from that of many other Shakespearean plays, as the plot is rather limited in contrast with the scenic effects (the shipwreck, sea storm, and magic): "Despite the play's unique panoply of visual wonders, very little happens on Prospero's enchanted island. . . . A sense of newness, of wonder, of exciting discovery nonetheless pervades the play,

---

[17] Theatre without Borders is an informal initiative of scholars to discuss intercultural and transnational aspects of early modern theatre and drama. In addition to hosting annual conferences, it has published various books on this matter. See its website, https://sites.gallatin.nyu.edu/theaterwithoutborders/ (accessed February 24, 2023).

transcending its restricted geography and paucity of action" (Vaughan and Vaughan 1999: 4).

Indeed, beginning with the storm – whose representation on the allegedly bare Elizabethan stage seems to be somehow sober to us – the integration of wondrous and magical elements marks the plot of the play. The banquet scene (3.3.17–82) opens the basic level of the play to a more allegorical experience. This break in the mode of representation is remarked on by the characters themselves: "A living drollery!" (3.3.21). Ariel's metamorphosis into a harpy (3.3.53) is evaluated by Prospero in the appreciative tone of true connoisseur: "Bravely the figure of this harpy hast thou / Performed, my Ariel; a grace it had, devouring" (3.3.83–4).

The dramaturgy of the play is so complex because not all metatheatrical scenes are on the same level: although Prospero describes the magical scenes, too, as a performance of Ariel's, the genuinely staged scene of the masque (4.1.59–142) is framed as a spectacle set for the attendance of Ferdinand and Miranda.

Because they have often been added in the process of printing the text, stage directions are not strong evidence in early modern plays (Dessen 2009), but it is clear that *The Tempest* calls for the full possibilities of the stage: notes "on the top" (*Tempest* III.3.19 f.) as well as on some form of machinery indicate that these effects are not meant to be achieved by acting alone.

This becomes even more evident if we look at post-Restoration adaptations of the play. In 1667, William Davenant and John Dryden added the subtitle *Enchanted Island*, which carried the play through the eighteenth and well into the nineteenth century. Their version smooths some of Shakespeare's plotlines (e.g., by adding a sister for Miranda). But it also responds to a more elaborate theatrical apparatus, incorporating a masque of Neptune and Amphitrite and – according to the stage directions – actually *depicting* the sinking of the ship, accompanied by singing: "Ariel and other spirits assisting the Storm" (Shakespeare 1790: 53, 11 [qtd.]). The depiction of ships, especially in heavy weather, has been a staple effect in stage machinery since the seventeenth century: Nicola Sabbatini (1574–1654) published an extensive tract on these techniques, showing a ship in moving waves (Figure 33).

The reception of the Davenant/Dryden version was fueled mainly by its transformation into a full opera by Thomas Shadwell and Thomas Betterton

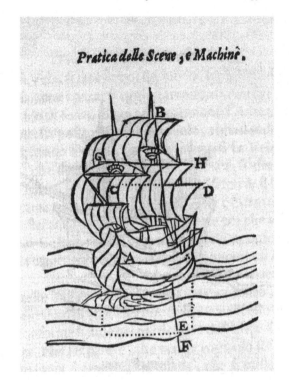

Figure 33 N. Sabbatini: Stage machinery for a ship at sea. Permission of Theaterwissenschaftliche Sammlung/University of Cologne.

in 1674. As T. Sofie Taubert (2018: 73) has argued, the popularity of the Shakespearean plot in the (late) eighteenth century, both in England and on the continent, rested on the intrinsic connection between the concept of wonder and the usage of music. The sensation of music makes up for fallacies in the logic of the plot.

According to Taubert (2018: 95–133), the lavish stage presentation of storms, earthquakes, shipwrecks, and other catastrophes in *The Tempest* and its adaptations deploys an amalgamation of music, scenes of magic, and a complex technical apparatus. These currents are also particularly strong in peep-box sheets (Figures 34 and 35). More than simply theatregrams, such sheets are small scenarios in which the spectacle provided by the technical apparatus has become the leading dramaturgical element.

This tendency can be well observed in a German adaptation of *The Tempest*: *Die Geisterinsel* (*The Spirits' Island*) by Friedrich Wilhelm Gotter (1746–97) was originally written for the composer Johann Friedrich Anton Fleischmann (1766–98) and premiered in Frankfurt am Main in 1792. This version expands the storyline to include the conflict between the "evil witch" Sycorax – who is merely mentioned in Shakespeare's play as Caliban's mother – and the goddess Maja (Taubert 2018: 81–3). Interwoven with the plotlines known from Shakespeare, this cosmic conflict between Maja and Sycorax culminates in a pantomimic act 3, scene 2.

A thunderstorm breaks loose, the earth is cracked open, and Sycorax, described as "schwarzer Schatten" (black shadow), appears and turns belligerently toward the tomb of Maja. The tomb bursts into pieces, and Maja – "ein weisser Schatten" (white shadow) – appears. They silently battle each other, Maja turns to heaven, thunder and lightning appear again, and Sycorax vanishes into the ground under flames, while Maja returns to her grave, the tomb supplanted by a palm tree (Gotter 1797b: 56). Clearly, this scene is mostly a blueprint to deploy the stage machinery but also to include popular effects. While critics were mostly unsatisfied by the scene because it felt out of place, its appearance in various musical adaptations of the libretto is proof of its more general popularity (Taubert 2018: 118).

Robert Greene's (1558–1592) *Friar Bacon and Friar Bungay* (c. 1589) (hereafter FB&FB) addresses the question of magic and wonder explicitly. The key protagonist, Friar Bacon (who echoes the historical figure of Roger Bacon, 1219–92), represents the characteristic tension of the *magia naturalis*: a mixture of early sciences, alchemy, and esoteric worldview. The plot around Friar Bacon is intertwined with a love plot, in which Edward, Prince of Wales, and his friend Lacy both fall in love with Margaret, daughter of the keeper of the village Fressingfield. This love plot, which eventually comes to a happy ending, is carried out in an almost mechanical way; the psychological depiction of the characters is rather rough.

Figure 34 Peep-box sheet: Quake of Messina (1785). Permission of Theaterwissenschaftliche Sammlung University of Cologne/Sammlung Werner Nekes (joint ownership: University of Cologne/DFF/Filmmuseum Potsdam).

Although Lacy has promised to woo Margaret for Edward, he spontaneously falls in love with her and urges her to marry him right away. In scene 6, this encounter is portrayed in parallel with one of Edward, who watches the lovers thanks to a "magic mirror" provided by Bacon. But Edward does not just passively observe the scene; he begs Bacon to intervene on his behalf, which Bacon does by striking dumb (silencing) Friar Bungay, who is about to officiate the wedding of Lacy and Margaret. Eventually, Bacon conjures a devil to bring Bungay to him.

Dramaturgically, this scene is interesting because of its poly-scenic order: it represents not a unified field of vision but a double scene that is intertwined in the plot (Freebury-Jones 2022: 51). The "magic mirror" is

Figure 35 Sea storm scene in an Engelbrecht perspective theatre. Permission of Theaterwissenschaftliche Sammlung University of Cologne/Sammlung Werner Nekes (joint ownership: University of Cologne/DFF/Filmmuseum Potsdam)/Photo Hermann & Clärchen Baus.

not merely a metaphor for a telescope; in addition to providing image and sound, it enables Bacon to intervene in the scene and stop the ceremony. While a comparable object is used by John Webster (c. 1580–c. 1634) in *The White Devil* (1612) (*White Devil* II.2.1–23), Greene exploits the possibilities of a poly-scenic stage in an even more radical way: the magical tool is a central dramaturgical device that organizes the narrative structure and the spatial arrangement.

But magic appears in two further ways in the play. The first is a subplot in scene 9, involving a public competition between Dr. Jacques Vandermast (a magician in the entourage of the Habsburg emperor) and the two friars (first Bungay and later Bacon). What starts as a scholarly dispute about the power of different kinds of magic soon evolves into a competitive display, as the stage directions note: "Bungay utters his spell and a golden tree rises from the ground, with a dragon in its branches, spitting out fire. Friar Bungay steps back and Vandermast comes forward" (FB&FB 9.42).

This golden tree is identified by Bungay as the tree of the Hesperides, from which Hercules, killing the guardian dragon, steals the golden apples. Accordingly, Vandermast conjures Hercules and orders him to cut down the tree and kill the dragon. "By the side of the tree, appears the figure of Hercules, wearing his lion's skin. . . . Hercules begins to tear down the branches from Bungay's golden tree" (FB&FB 9.43). When Vandermast challenges Bungay to order Hercules to stop, the friar is defeated.

In this moment, Bacon appears and mocks Vandermast. He binds Hercules to such an extent that the conjured figure does not dare obey Vandermast's spells: "I dare not. See's thou not great Bacon here, Whose frown doth act more than thy magic can?" (FB&FB 9.44). Eventually, Bacon commands Hercules to take Vandermast away:

> *Hercules sieʒes Vandermast with one hand and the tree with the other, and all vanish.*
>
> Emp[eror]. Why, Bacon, whither dost thou send him?
> Bac[on]. To Habsburg, there your highness in return
>   Shall find the German in his study. (FB&FB 9.45)

Although we have no proper hint as to how this scene was produced onstage, some kind of apparatus must have been at hand.

The second, most prominent element of magic in the play is the Brazen Head, which Bacon has constructed as a kind of oracle over seven years. In scene 11, Bacon commands his famulus, Miles, to watch over the head and wake Bacon up as soon as it speaks. As soon as Bacon is asleep, the head starts to talk: "TIME is. . . . TIME was. . . . TIME is PAST." "*Then there is a flash of lightning and a hand appears, which breaks the Head with a hammer*" (FB&FB 9.56).

The theatrical effect of the speaking head was so strong that it appeared as an image on the front page of the 1655 quarto edition (Figure 36). But the prominence of the Brazen Head as an object comes not only from Greene's play. As mentioned earlier, a "brasen hed . . . which dyd seme to speak" figures as one of the key examples in John Dee's (1570: n.p.) list of thaumaturgical objects. The motif of the speaking Brazen Head was already part of the popular tale *The Famous Historie of Fryer Bacon* (oldest printed version, 1627), which clearly was used by Greene as material for his play. While in its references the play is very faithful to the legend, the motif itself is rather evocative in numerous ways, particularly recalling the legend of Albert the Great and his speaking image (Scheeben 1932: 206–7).

What might appear as a lack from the literary point of view gains additional meaning if we take Greene's depiction of magic into account. That is, the magical wonders and tools are "real," not illusionary or

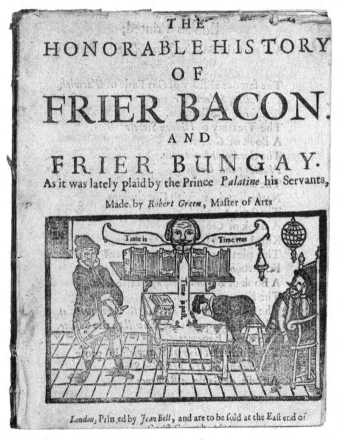

Figure 36 Robert Greene (1558?–92). The honorable history of Frier Bacon and Frier Bungay (London: [J. Bell], 1655), title page. Call #: G1828. Used by permission of the Folger Shakespeare Library.

limited to internal effects, like the love potion in *A Midsummer Night's Dream*. Rather, they have a scenic presence and are acknowledged as real by the other characters. The Brazen Head does speak; Vandermast is brought back to Germany; Lacy and Margaret confess their love to each other.

To describe this phenomenon, Jenny Sager (2013: 106), drawing from Tom Gunning's (1990) notion of a "cinema of attraction," identified Greene's plays as a "theatre of attraction," defined by the "use of unique visual attractions or curiosities to attract the attention of the audience and to incite speculation." Sager's argument helps clarify the dramaturgical organization of Greene's play. It is not so much character-focused as it is fueled and driven by the presentation of thaumaturgical apparatuses and tricks. The play is document to an existing media practice that has been put at the center of a narrative construction.

Apparatuses as the DNA of Scripts

But where Greene's play centers thaumaturgical apparatuses in its dramaturgy, other plays simply make use of such effects to unfold and develop their narrative plot.

Sometimes, the integration of or allusion to a media form can be a single dramaturgical effect, as in Shakespeare's *The Winter's Tale* (1611). Leontes's encounter with the "statue" of Hermione is orchestrated by comments from Paulina that frame the encounter like a thaumaturgical act:

> PAULINA. Either forbear,
> 	Quit presently the chapel, or resolve you
> 	For more amazement. If you can behold it,
> 	I'll make the statue move indeed; descend,
> 	And take you by the hand. But then you'll think –
> 	(Which I protest against) I am assisted
> 	By wicked powers.
> LEONTES. What you can make her do
> 	I am content to look on: what to speak,
> 	I am content to hear; for 'tis as easy

                    To make her speak as move.
PAULINA It is requir'd
                    You do awake your faith. Then, all stand still:
                    Or – those that think it is unlawful business
                    I am about, let them depart. (*Winter's Tale* V.5.85–97)

Shakespeare clearly evokes a thaumaturgical performance of automata or
puppets, and the vivification of Hermione is a *coup de théâtre* that resonates
with the various versions of the Pygmalion myth. In this episode from
Ovid's *Metamorphoses*, the sculptor Pygmalion falls in love with one of his
statues. In response to his pleas, Venus turns her into a human being.
Shakespeare's moving statue quotes automata to create further momentum
for his dramaturgical effect: the actor mimics a statue, thereby creating an
ironic double play on statues mimicking living persons.

A different inclusion of media apparatuses can be found in Ben
Jonson's (1572–1637) *Bartholomew Fair* (1614). Jonson's play features
a dispute about the antitheatrical campaigns driven by radical Protestant
forces. Jonson not only presents a puppet show as a play within the play
but even has the Puritan character Zeal-of-the-Land Busy interact with
and dispute a puppet. After a quick stichomythia between Busy and the
puppet, Busy draws on an argument against the theatre as an abomination
because of the cross-dressing of actors:

          Bus[y]. Yes, and my main argument against you is, that you are an
                    abomination; for the male, among you, putteth on the apparel
                    of the *Female*, and the *Female* of the *Male*.
          Pup[pet]. D[onisius]. [Puppet Dionysius]. *You lye, you lye, you lye
                    abominably.*
          Cok[es]. Good, by my troth, he has given him the lye thrice.
          Pup[pet]. D[onisius]. *It is your old stale argument against the Players,
                    but it will not hold against the Puppets; for we have neyther
                    Male nor Female amongst us. And that thou may'st see, if thou
                    wilt, like a malicious purblinde ʒeale as thou art.*
                                        [The Puppet takes up his garment.]

Edg[worth]. By my faith, there he has answer'd you, friend; a playne
    demonstration.

Pup[pet]. D[onisius]. *Nay, I'le prove, against ere a* Rabbin *of 'hem all,
    that my standing is as lawfull as his; that I speak by inspira-
    tion, as well as he; that I have as little to doe with learning as
    he; and doe scorn her helps as much as he.*

Bus[y]. I am confuted, the *Cause* hath failed me.

Pus. [*sic*] *Then be converted, be converted.*

Lan[t Leatherhead]. Be converted, I pray you, and let the play goe on!

Busy. Let it go on; for I am changed, and will become a beholder
    with you. (*Bartholomew Fair* V.5: 128f.; emphasis in the
    original)

Jonson has not accidentally put this dispute – and the ostentatious conver-
sion of the Puritan Busy – into a play that conjures the vibrant social
environment of the Bartholomew Fair: theatre performances, other holiday
pastimes, and sports. The fair enjoyed the support and patronage of the
court but not of city authorities and thus became another site of the
controversy between the court and the Puritans. *Bartholomew Fair*,
a drama written for the king's entertainment on All Saints' Night, makes
a play of the city's own festival (McEvoy 2008: 121).

Kristina E. Caton (2013: 70) puts this argument even further, suggesting
that the puppet raises fundamental questions about subjectivity and identity
vis-à-vis the material world: "Fittingly, Jonson [chose] the puppet theatre to
explore the many intersections between agency and materiality since it was
a well-known site for satirical treatment of the institutions, religious,
academic, economic, political, or familial, which claimed the right to
regulate both behaviour and thought."

The fact that, as Sean McEvoy (2008: 120) argues, a kind of fair was
probably built onstage for Jonson's play makes obvious that the abyssal line
that governs archival work (with its prejudice against puppetry) belies the
permeability of early modern media ecology (Caton 2013: 57–8). That it is
a puppet that successfully rebuts the Puritan's arguments is a good index for
the vitality of this pluralistic media ecology.

The play *The Travels of the Three English Brothers* (1607) (hereafter *Travels*), written by John Day (1574–c. 1638), William Rowley (c. 1585–1626), and George Wilkins (1576–1618), exemplifies a different kind of dramatic text, one that uses thaumaturgical elements as part of its narrative structure. Based on a 1607 pamphlet by Anthony Nixon (1592–1616), the play portrays the lives of brothers Anthony, Thomas, and Robert Shirley, three well-known adventurers and travelers. It places their lives in the conflict between the Persian and the Ottoman empires, also depicting the politics of the English Crown in these Mediterranean conflicts.

Notwithstanding questions of topicality and the political implications of the play, its dramaturgical structure is interesting because it is clearly driven by a nondramatic narrative. Thus, the play's plot depends on cuts and jumps between faraway locations and various moments, mediated/narrated in an at-times proto-Brechtian, alienating manner. Right at the beginning, when Robert and Anthony encounter the Sophy (Shah) of Persia, who is about to go to battle with the Ottoman sultan, the play integrates two mock battles:

> A battle presented. Excursion; the one half drive out the other, then enter with heads on their swords. (*Travels* I.48f.)

> A Christian battle shown between the two brothers. ROBERT driven out, then enter SIR ANTHONY and the rest with the other part prisoners. (*Travels* I.87–9)

The two mock battles introduce a leading topic of the play: the question of clemency and the taking of prisoners (instead of executing the defeated). But they also establish another element, this one related to the question of fireworks: the presentation of cannons. The Sophy describes the "Christian battle" first and foremost as an aesthetic experience:

> Your wars are royal,
> So joined with music that even death itself
> Would seem a dream; your instruments dissolve

A body into spirit but to hear
Their cheerful clamours; and those your engines –
We cannot give their proper character –
Those loud tongues that spit their spleen in fire,
Drowning the groans of your then-dying friends. (*Travels* I.89–96)

As a subsequent stage direction indicates, the cannons were actually fired onstage: "Chambers go off" (*Travels* I.118). While the historical recounting presented here, with its claim that non-European empires were not familiar with artillery, is historically wrong and indicative of the emerging Occidental discourse of hegemony, we can see how the close intertwining of pyrotechnics and artillery presents cannons as spectacle. They are also widely used in other scenes of the play.

The presentation of mock battles as well as cannons within the play has to be seen as a dramaturgical decision in its own right: while Shakespeare's *Henry V* (1599) begins with a lamentation that the stage ("this unworthy scaffold"; prologue 11) is not able to present battles convincingly, here the play makes an effort to do so, even putting this presentation at the center of its dramaturgical structure.

Clearly, the attempt to create a scenic version of Nixon's pamphlet leads to an expansion of the dramatical scena. Thaumaturgical elements and the display of media are indispensable tools in this process. This becomes true in the brief pantomime at the end of the play. *Fame* as chorus sums up the further events in his epilogue but also presents the following scene, recounted in the stage directions:

> Enter three several ways the three brothers: ROBERT with the state of Persia as before; SIR ANTHONY with the King of Spain and others, where he receives the Order of Saint Iago, and other offices; SIR THOMAS in England, with his father and others. FAME gives to each a prospective glass: they seem to see one another and offer to embrace, at which FAME parts them, and so exeunt all except FAME. (*Travels* XIII.14ff.)

As an editor's note remarks, the "prospective glass" here is "traditionally a magical device for seeing distant or future events" (*Travels* 133). While the "magic mirror" in Greene's *Friar Bacon and Friar Bungay* is provided by Bacon as a magical device, the prospective glass is part of the scenic apparatus. In this sense, we can read the concluding dumb show not only as an illustration of the epilogue but also as a kind of metatheatrical comment on the poly-scenic nature of the scena envisioned by this play.

Reading dramatic literature through the prism of early modern media ecology offers a dual perspective. On the one hand, nontextual influences and factors like apparatuses or their effects become visible. They might become topical as elements of magic or merely serve the dramaturgical structure. On the other hand, the presence of other forms of media allows us to better understand the politics of genre formation: poetological ideals do not merely propagate aesthetic ideals but can be understood as governing the volatile social sphere of media ecology.

Cartographing Early Modern Media Ecology and Its Study

As the discussion thus far has shown, early modern media ecology calls for a fresh approach that takes into account the multiple facets of this culture. In the following, I try to discern certain hallmarks of the period more clearly: its polyglotism, polycentrism, polyphony, and polymorphism as well as its tendency of connection and permeability. I will take each of these in turn.

Polyglotism

The European early modern period spoke in many tongues: sometimes simultaneously, sometimes hierarchically structured, and sometimes with the pure joy of variation and different registers. Whereas modern Western historiography, obliged to the idea of the nation-state, departs from the idea of a confluence of territory, people, language, and culture, the early modern period did not run on such ideas of homogeneity. On the contrary, polyglotism was a hallmark of its social and cultural structure: there existed formally sanctioned linguæ francæ, such as Latin for learned discourse and, after the Thirty Years' War, French for court life. Vernaculars also gained importance at this time, fueled by the Protestant Reformation.

But the linguistic corridors of the early modern period did not run along today's national borders. To give just two examples: speakers of Low German were able to communicate across the borders of Germany and the Netherlands; Flemish and the Ripuarian dialect were well understood in provinces of today's Belgium and the Netherlands (Elmentaler and Voeste 2019).

The phenomenon of the *Wandertruppen* (touring troupes) – most prominently Dutch, English, and Italian – has caused some consternation among scholars because most of these troupes performed in their respective mother tongues. But linguistic comprehension obviously was not the major issue that it has been assumed to be, and this was not only because of the spectacular stagings: the highly mobile and transcultural performance and media practices created multiple "contact zones" (Pratt 1992), fostering improvised audience comprehension. While linguistic differences constitute a problem for a primarily literary culture, the actors and performers in this media ecology managed to find and reach their audience, linguistic competencies notwithstanding.

Polycentrism

The Western paradigm of spatial order, since the nineteenth century formulated as the nation-state, is based on the idea of one center that epitomizes the dominion. Following modernity's *grand récit* – departing from the French Revolution as its point of birth – France can be considered the ideal of this cultural logic. Paris epitomizes the concept of a metropolis, influencing the periphery in political, economic, cultural, social, and intellectual matters. Yet back projections of this logic miss the point that France (or England, for that matter) was not paradigmatic of the political system of the early modern period. In contrast, the quintessentially polycentric Holy Roman Empire, with its roughly 300–350 princely courts, 70 clerical residencies, and 50 free imperial cities, could be taken as a paradigm (Sittig 2012: xxxiii).

To complicate things even further, there is not a single parameter by which centers were defined in this era. Performers of all sorts traveled along the trade routes and offered their wares, often at the same venues and on the same occasions as other tradespeople: fairs and marketplaces were as ideal for the exchange of images, tales, and sensations as they were for the exchange of material goods. Printing, on the other hand, allowed for a remote relation of production and reception, facilitating networks of diasporic communities but also distant connections among places. Last but not least were political events, coronations, weddings, and royal entries, all of which provided opportunities for performances of all sorts.

Thus, any approach to the early modern condition must take this complex, constantly changing, and sometimes confusing structure seriously. Whereas the era of modern capitalism condensed activities to key metropolises and centers of engagement, the polycentric structure of the early modern era highlighted the importance of networks. These networks could be formalized – like the Hanseatic League, religious orders, or political treatises – or they could be informal, based on economic principles (trade routes, fairs, etc.) or simply shared interests. Regardless of their formality, their spheres and ways of circulation usually piggybacked on existing structures: printing, marketplaces, trade routes, performance opportunities, small-scale trade, and religious and political occasions.

Clearly, these networks, whether formalized or fragile and impromptu, were not bound to the European continent. On the contrary, early modern media ecology fostered the phenomenon that Subrahmanyam (1997: 745; and see 2019: 319–23) has described as *connected histories*. Early modern media ecology is a field marked by the multiple connections that can be found between societies and political systems. Its products and phenomena traveled on galleys, on oxcart, in caravans, and on foot. The flow of ideas, images, stories, and sensations was probably slower and more labor-intensive than in the period of a "globalized theatre" (Balme 2019), but the connections fostered the growth of a transcultural imagery. Digital humanities offers an innovative way for us to begin to trace these connections in early modern media ecology: the methodological approach known as *network analysis*, which allows for large-scale investigation of a corpus (Rotger, Roig-Sanz, and Puxan-Oliva 2019).

Polyphony

The system of the arts and media was less clearly organized in the early modern period than we might assume today. Despite the "rediscovery" of Aristotle in the seventeenth century and the quickly emerging poetological and aesthetic discourses, forms and genres were changing and merging in this period. As discussed in the "Dramatic Echoes" section, we must not think of the early modern drama as a fixed literary work of art that preceded and governed its performance. The same holds true for the visual culture, whose vitality was driven by a constant mixing and mingling, as Caroline van Eck and Stijn Bussels (2010: 214) have stated: "The boundaries between genres, media and arts; and virtually every use of theatrical elements presented here [raise] questions about the relations between works of art and their viewers, and about how the work of art stages the act of viewing."

The concept of media ecology allows us to take this recognition of polyphony a step further, viewing early modern media and forms of art as elements in a continuum of artistic representation that was still in the process of being shaped.

Polymorphism

Many still-prevalent theoretical discourses on media are bound to the idea of an ever-perfecting imitation of the world. Media history in its technocentric form is particularly written along these lines, conveniently ending with the emergence of photography and film as core examples of realism. Even Jay David Bolter and Richard Grusin (1999: 21–44), whose concept of remediation was developed to thwart the teleological foundation of media history, assume that the invisibility of the medium is what drives any development.

But things are more complicated: in *Techniques of the Observer* (1992), Jonathan Crary discusses the development of the camera obscura from the sixteenth century onward. This apparatus was based on the phenomenon in which a small hole in a dark chamber would create an image of light (though in reverse) on the opposite wall (Figure 37). Crary (1992: 36) argues that, although the same physical principles underpin photography, "what separates photography from both perspective and the camera obscura is far more significant than what they have in common." His point of departure is an analysis of the writings of Italian polymath Giambattista della Porta (1535–1615). One of the first scholars to describe the camera obscura, della Porta was indifferent to the question of whether the apparatus shows "reality" or "illusion" (Crary 1992: 37n26; and see Zambelli 2007; Kodera 2012). Thus, Crary deconstructs a popular master narrative of Western media history that inevitably leads to photography and film as the vanishing point of media development.

Acknowledging the polymorphic nature of media ecology means realizing that various principles of representation could occur in the same historical moment and might even be in dialogue or competition with one another. This formal pluralism corresponded with an ability among spectators to perceive these different forms accordingly. Instead of presumptuously assuming that past spectators were naïve and easy to

Figure 37 Camera obscura. In: A. Kircher, Amsterdam, 2nd ed., 1671, *Ars Magna Lucis et Umbræ*, p. 709. Permission of Theaterwissenschaftliche Sammlung University of Cologne/Sammlung Werner Nekes (joint ownership: University of Cologne/DFF/Filmmuseum Potsdam).

fool, we should research the foundations and training processes of these diversified grammars, building up to a complex *ars spectandi* (art/way of spectating).

While the concept of an ever-refining realism eclipses many forms within the Western tradition, it had an even more restrictive effect toward non-Occidental traditions, often disputing their status as "art." The concept of media ecology allows us to acknowledge these alternative forms of representation. Instead of assuming an intrinsic, quasi-evolutionary tendency toward Realism, we gain a glimpse of varying intentions. Metin And (1963: 11), the authority on Turkish theatre, argued, for example, that Islamic authorities accepted the Turkish Karagöz shadow plays because of their explicitly non-naturalistic form:

> Theologians had to make another concession to general usage in the traditional Turkish shadow theatre, also popular in Egypt and Tunisia, for Karagöz and other characters. The law forbade the imitation of living beings as rivalling God's exclusive power to create. But the shadow puppets were proven to be inanimate. The nature of the design helped serve as an excuse, for the puppet, attached by a string or rod through a hole which transmitted the light, could hardly be mistaken for human flesh.

The nonrealism of Karagöz is not at all an exception. On the contrary, art in the Persian cosmopolis (on this term, see Flatt 2019: 17–24) showed a comparable reservation against realistic depictions and rather favored an ostensible anti-illusionism (Minissale 2007). The painting *Jahangir Preferring a Sufi Shaikh to Kings* (1615–18, Figure 38), by seventeenth-century Indian artist Bichitr, shows the Mughal emperor Jahangir being visited by four men: a Sufi, a sultan, the English king James, and the artist himself.

The artist presents each of the figures in a different style of painting. As Kavita Singh (2017: 70) writes, King James (third figure from the left) is presented in a rather realistic but seemingly less accomplished style:

Figure 38 Bichitr (1615–40), "Jahangir Preferring a Sufi Shaikh to Kings, from the St. Peterburg Album", F1942.15a, edanmdm:fsg F1942.15a, Smithsonian Institution, Washington, D.C., National Museum of Asian Art, Freer Gallery of Art Collection.

In the Mughal artist's paintings, this was manifested by an aesthetic of interruptions, where the eye, led smoothly into a passage of illusionistic representation, was then deliberately stopped short as it was confronted with a passage of stylized imagery or flat patterning. Through this technique, the artist could simultaneously display his tremendous command over painterly skills and show his awareness of what his skill produced: an illusion, marks on paper.

In much this way, the simultaneity and juxtaposition of varying grammars of representation exemplify the polymorphic character of premodern media ecology, in which different registers coexisted and served – in various contexts – different aesthetic, intellectual, and strategic purposes.

Connection and Permeability

Given the historical circumstances in northern Europe, where the period from 1450 to 1800 was determined by continual fights for predominance, the extent to which Western societies and cultures were in constant exchange and dialogue, particularly with Asian societies and states, is sometimes overlooked. While it has been argued that "globalization" as a process is rooted in Western political hegemony (and military presence), a capitalist economy, and a modern technology that allows for fast and constant forms of connection (such as the steamship or the telegraph), the premodern world was in a comparable way connected and permeable.

As discussed in the "Minds, Hands, and Heads" section, agents in this process of mediation could be either individual actors (merchants, mercenaries, and adventurers) or representatives of larger organizations (missionaries and diplomats). They might be part of an official structure (following or being commanded by various forms of protocol), or else they could form an instantaneous, volatile structure, in most cases rather tolerated than accepted, in the form of "liberated zones" as Boaventura de Sousa Santos (2018: 31) describes them: "consensual communities, based on participation of all their members. They are of a performative, prefigurative, and educational nature."

A comprehensive perspective on these questions of permeability has to acknowledge the diversity of connecting points and connecting strategies: circulation could be based on economic, political, intellectual, or aesthetic premises (see Marx 2021a). We must not romanticize the idea of wandering troupes and circulating techniques but rather meticulously follow the trade routes and channels through which they moved.

Media history is a history of migration, and in the European context, it was the Savoyards (so named for the Alpine region of Savoy) who became the epitome of traveling media: "roaming storytellers, peddlers, and performers ... [who] became magic lantern showmen" (Lipton 2021: 16). While probably only a minority of performers actually came from Savoy, the term *Savoyard* became a name for all *Fahrende* (vagabond artists) (see Füsslin et al. 1995: 36–45; Lipton 2021: 17–19).[18] To acknowledge this migratory history means to realize that most protagonists remain(ed) nameless and faceless. The history of media ecology, then, cannot be written as a history of great (White) men; it can be written only by carefully tracing the footsteps and residues of those who lent their feet and backs, their lifetimes, and well-being to the flourishing of these ephemeral arts.

A 1720 caricature from Nicolo Cantabella (Figure 39) shows – deliberately distorting the figure of the carrier – one such peep-box presenter (or *Guckkästner*). Particularly revealing here is not only this central figure but rather the image's decorative frame, which offers a glimpse into the complexity and interconnectedness of this media ecology. At the bottom of the page, we find a stereotypical representation of a Chinese opium smoker, holding a teacup in his right hand and an opium pipe in his left. While there is no specific reason for the Chinese figure, it represents the era's general taste for exoticism. The column on the left presents dice, a she-donkey with a bonnet, and theatrical masks, and below this is an object that could represent a wine bottle; whereas the column on the right presents – below the dice – a monkey in costume, masks, flutes, and a gigantic sausage. Taken together, these objects refer to the fair spectacles and the insatiable

---

[18] Nandini Das and colleagues (2021) have shown how in English law, the term *vagabond* became a general category for all who lived in mobility and were suspicious to the authorities.

Figure 39 Caricature of a peep-box presenter by N. Cantabella (c. 1720). Permission of Theaterwissenschaftliche Sammlung University of Cologne/ Sammlung Werner Nekes (joint ownership: University of Cologne/DFF/ Filmmuseum Potsdam).

appetite of the harlequinesque figures of the wandering comedians. In this sense, the caricature represents a kaleidoscope of those neighboring art forms and representations that came with the Savoyards.

Postscriptum: A History of Clouds

It is jammed. The mechanism is jammed, and instead of gracefully and smoothly floating, the clouds stutter and stammer. Yet, for some, even this mutilated trick is a soul-shattering revelation: "I am no longer Coviello. I'm a body without a soul, completely beside myself. I no longer care for this world. You too, beware: don't start longing to see Master Graziano's things" (Bernini 1985: 54).

Admittedly, exaggeration is part of the comedy's design, but the impressive effects are partly testified for by other figures. Except one: Master Graziano. He is not only disappointed but outright infuriated at the mishap of his technicians: "Damn you all, stage machines aren't to make people laugh, but to make them gaze in wonder. Who the hell's going to marvel at this contraption? You don't have to be brilliant to see it's only good for a laugh" (Bernini 1985: 52).

Clearly, Graziano has a vision – one that painfully hits the reality of his stagehands. So he desperately declares:

> I want my cloud standing out, detached against the blue, and visible in all its dimensions like a real cloud up in the air. . . .
> Ingenuity and design constitute the Magic Art by whose means you deceive the eye and make your audience gaze in wonder, make a cloud stand out against the horizon then float downstage, still free, with a natural motion. Gradually approach the viewer, it will seem to dilate, to grow larger and larger. The wind will seem to waft it, waveringly, here and there, then up, higher and higher – not just haul it in place, bang, with a counterweight. (Bernini 1985: 53)

Graziano's ideal exceeds the limitations of the regular stage machine. And since the text is a fragment, we know not whether Graziano succeeds in his art. Yet what is evident is that Graziano's aesthetic ideals fall into the category of *thaumaturgy*: making people "gaze in wonder." The author of the short dramatic sketch is legendary Italian sculptor Gian Lorenzo Bernini (1598–1680), and Graziano – modeled after the *commedia dell'arte* mask of the Dottore (Figure 40) – is clearly his alter ego (Lavin 1964: 570).[19] Bernini was closely involved in various theatrical activities, especially around Carnival, and was famous for his stage effects. In 1638, he staged an event that included a flooding of the stage: at the event's peak, the barriers seemed to break, threatening to flood the auditorium, only to have the crisis averted at the last minute. Even more spectacular was an effect he used various times in which a clumsy torchbearer came too close to the painted canvas of the scenery, setting it on fire (see Warwick 2012: 33).

The cloud that Graziano dreams of has a similar effect of amazement, but first and foremost, it epitomizes Bernini's ideal of a seemingly effortless effect. Indeed, Bernini's concept of theatre was not specifically machine-based; he sought immediate effects with simple means (Lavin 2007: 19–20).

Clouds were, of course, a well-established scenic decoration as early as the Middle Ages (Buccheri 2014). Yet most of these apparatuses were built around painted clouds, moved by a mechanical system similar to the one ridiculed by Graziano (Figure 41).

The cloud is more than an element of the environment, like the ocean; it connotes a spiritual level. Its depiction in churches signified transcendence. When, for example, after the Council of Trent (1545–63), the veneration of the Eucharist gained increasing importance, it was often presented framed by a triumphal arch of clouds (Buccheri 2014, 169–70). But clouds also signaled secular transcendence in decorations of the appearance of the deus (or dea) ex machina (Figure 42). As elaborate as these machines were, they always remained limited by the mechanisms on which they were built.

Graziano, in contrast, envisions a simpler yet more daring solution: a three-dimensional cloud as it appears in nature, displaying the ambivalence of being a material object yet of ethereal quality. This cloud figures as

[19] I thank Odai Johnson for drawing my attention to Bernini's play.

LE DOCTOR BALOARD

Figure 40 J. J. Wolrab: Figurine of the Dottore (c. 1720). Permission of Theaterwissenschaftliche Sammlung/University of Cologne.

the utopian focal point of early modern thaumaturgy: setting the spectators in amazement through its appearance but also challenging the categories of perception and cosmology. Although Viktoria Tkaczyk (2011: 240–65) has

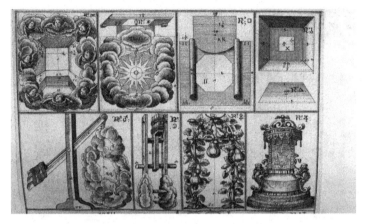

Figure 41 Machines to present clouds on stage. In: J. Furttenbach, Augsburg, 1663, *Mannhaffter Kunst-Spiegel*, p. 46. Permission of Theaterwissenschaftliche Sammlung/University of Cologne.

shown that the depiction of clouds on the early modern stage had only very few connections to the emerging meteorological discourse, the clouds as a spectacular object open a transgressive dimension to the scena of the early modern period.

Whereas Athanasius Kircher's metamorphosis machine blurred the idea of self-reflection, Graziano-Bernini's vision of the miraculous cloud onstage draws attention to the world in the broadest sense of the word. The material yet ephemeral "reality" makes an appearance on the early modern scena. In this sense, we can read Bernini's play as a primal scene for writing the history of early modern media ecology, for writing a history of clouds. On the one hand, it is driven by the ambivalence and connection of *materiality and ephemerality*. In contrast to the painted and mechanical clouds of the theatrical apparatus, Graziano's vision is utopian yet real in the sense of demarcating the historical place of these images, which clearly appeared but left no material residue – like the firework, the magic lantern image, or the shadow. Grasping their historical dimension challenges us to embrace both

Figure 42 L. Burnacini, sketch to a scene of *Il pomo d'oro*: "The Emotion –
Dance of the Heroes" (Vienna, 1668). Engraving. Permission of
Theaterwissenschaftliche Sammlung/University of Cologne.

sides: the material/technical condition as well as the ethereal appearance
and its conditions and interpretations. On the other hand, it rests on
a *semantic ambiguity* that invokes mythical as well as cosmological and
scientific categories.

   Graziano as an actor of this media practice represents both major forces:
he feels the despair of gravity, the painful recognition that his aesthetic ideas
are firmly limited by the material conditions of his art. Yet he also represents
a longing and a desire that do not take these limitations for the last word.
His heavens are neither empty nor reduced to a specific doctrine. To dream
of the open sky and the heavens above, with all means and despite all the
clumsiness of the technologies, is what is at the heart of early modern media
ecology.

Bibliography

Primary Sources

Agrippa von Nettesheim, H. C. (1564). *Henrici Cornelii Agrippae Ab Nettesheym, De Incertitvdine Et vanitate scientiarum declamatio inuectiua.* Lvgdvni.

Agrippa von Nettesheim, H. C. & French, J. (1651). *Three Books of Occult. Philosophy De Occulta Philosophia*, ed. R. W. for Gregory Moule. London: Gregory Moule.

[Al-Masudi], Maçoudi. (1865). *Les Praries D'or: Texte Et Traduction Par C. Barbier De Meynard. Tome Quatrième.* Paris: L'Imprimerie Impériale.

Arber, E., ed. (1868). *Edward Webb, Chief Master Gunner, His Traualies. 1590.* London: Alex. Murray & Son.

Bernini, G. L. (1985). *The Impresario. [Untitled]. Translated, with an Introduction and Notes, by Donald Beecher and Massimo Ciavolella.* Carleton Renaissance Plays in Translation. Ottawa: Dovehouse Editions Canada

Bochius J. (1595). *Descriptio publicae gratulationis, spectaculorum et ludorum, in adventu sereniss. principis Ernesti archiducis Austriae ...: an. M.D. XCIIII. XVIII. Kal. Iulias, aliisque diebus Antverpiae editorum; cui est praefixa, de Belgii principatu a Romano in ea provincia imperio ad nostra usque tempora brevis narratio.* Antwerp: Plantin.

Day, J., Rowley, W. & Wilkins, G. (1995). The Travels of the Three English Brothers. In Parr, A., ed., *Three English Travel Plays.* Manchester: Manchester University Press, pp. 55–134.

Doppelmayr, J. G. (1730). *Historische Nachricht von den Nürnbergischen Mathematicis und Künstlern.* Nuremberg: Peter Conrad Monath.

Du Halde, J. B. (1739). *The General History of China, Containing a Geographical, Historical, Chronological, Political and Physical*

Description of the Empire of China, Chinese-Tartary, Corea and Thibet. *Vol. III.* London: John Watt.

Ernst, J. D. (1697). *Auserlesene Gemüths-Ergetzligkeiten/Das ist: Funffzig sonderbare Lust- und Lehr-Gespräche: in welchen Von viel- und mancherley Historischen/ . . . Sachen . . . fürgestellet wird. Mit sonderbarem Fleiß also eingerichtet/ daß sie . . . nach Gelegenheiten nützlich zugebrauchen. Benebenst einen dreyfachen Register.* Magdeburg: Zeidlerische Schrifften.

Evliya Efendi [i.e. Çelebi] (1846). *Narrative Travels in Europe, Asia, and Africa in the Seventeenth Century. Vol. I, Part II.* London: The Oriental Translation Fund.

Fontana, J. (2014). *Liber Instrumentorum Iconographicus: Ein Illustriertes Maschinenbuch: Herausgegeben, übersetzt und eingeleitet von Horst Kranz.* Vol. LXVI of *Boethius: Texte und Abhandlungen zur Geschichte der Mathematik und Naturwissenschaften.* Stuttgart: Franz Steiner.

Gotter, F. W. (1797a). Die Geisterinsel: Ein Singspiel in drei Akten. (Teil 1). *Die Horen* 11(8), 1–26.

Gotter, F. W. (1797b). Die Geisterinsel: Ein Singspiel in drei Akten. (Teil 2). *Die Horen* 11(9), 1–78.

Greene, R. (2017). *Friar Bacon and Friar Bungay.* Whithorn: Anodos Books.

Griendel, J. F. (c. 1685). *Specificatio, Was Johann Frantz Griendl Von Ach Auf Wanckhausen/ Matthematicus Und Opticus in Nürnberg/ Von Optischen Raritäten Pfleget Zu Machen.* Nuremberg.

Hoogstraeten, S.v. (1678). *Inleyding tot de Hooge Schoole der Schilderkonst: Anders de Zichtbaere Werelt.* Rotterdam: Fransois van Hoogstraeten.

Jonson, B. (1904). *Bartholomew Fair. Edited with Introduction, Notes and Glossary by Carroll Storrs Alden.* New York: Henry Holt & Co.

Kircher, A. (1667). *Athanasii Kircheri E Soc. Jesu China Monumentis Qva Sacris quà Profanis, Nec non variis Naturæ & Artis Spectaculis, Aliarumque rerum memorabilium Argumentis Illustrata.* Amsterdam: Joannes Janssonius à Waesberge & Elizeus Weyerstraet.

Kircher, A. (1671). *Ars Magna Lucis et Umbræ*. 2nd ed. Amsterdam: Johannes Jansson.

Kircher, A. (2011). *Selbstbiographie: Aus dem Lateinischen übersetzt von Dr. Nikolaus Seng*. Petersberg: Michael Imhof Verlag.

Leibniz, G. W. (2006). *Der Briefwechsel mit den Jesuiten in China (1689–1714): Herausgegeben Von Rita Widmaier*. Hamburg: Felix Meiner.

Liudprand of Cremona & Becker, J. (1915). *Die Werke Liudprands Von Cremona*. Scriptores Rerum Germanicarum in Usum Scholarum Ex Monumentis Germaniae Historicis Separatim Editi Scriptores Rerum Germanicarum in Usum Scholarum Ex Monumentis Germaniae Historicis Recusi. Hannover: Hahn.

Nashe, T. (1594). *The Terrors of the Night: Or, the Discourse of Apparitions*. London: William Jones.

Patin, C. (1696). *Travels Thro Germany, Swisserland, Bohemia, Holland, and Other Parts of Europe*. London: A. Swall & T. Child.

Prynne, W. (1633). *Histrio-Mastix: The Players Scourge, or, Actors Tragaedie*. London: Michael Sparke.

Schott, C. (1677). *Magica Optica: Das ist Geheime doch Natur-mäßige Gesicht und Augenlehr*. Frankfurt/Main: Johan Martin Schönwetter.

Sepibus, G. d. (1678). *Romani Collegii Societatis Jesu Musaeum Celeberrimum: Cujus magnum Antiquariae rei, statuarum, imaginum, picturarumque partem Ex Legato Alphonsi Donini, … A Secretis, munificâ Liberalitate relictum; P. Athanasius Kircherus … novis & raris inventis locupletatum, compluriumque Principum curiosis donariis magno rerum apparatu instruxit*. Amsterdam: Jansson-Waesbergen.

Shakespeare, W. (1790). *The Tempest: Or, The Enchanted Island. Written by Shakespeare with additions from Dryden: as Compiled by J. P. Kemble. And First Acted at the Theatre-Royal Drury-Lane*. Dublin: George Perrin.

Shakespeare, W. (2011). *The Arden Shakespeare Complete Works*, rev. ed. Kastan, D.S., Proudfoot, G. R. & Thompson, A. London: Bloomsbury Methuen Drama.

Stieler, K. v. (1691). *Der teutschen Sprache Stammbaum und Fortwachs oder teutscher Sprachschatẓ* . . .. Nuremberg: Hofmann.

Webster, J. (2008). *The White Devil*, 3rd ed. Luckyj C. London: Methuen Drama.

Secondary Sources

Aebischer, P. (2020). *Shakespeare, Spectatorship and the Technologies of Performance*. Cambridge: Cambridge University Press.

Ágoston, G. (2005). *Guns for the Sultan: Military Power and the Weapons Industry in the Ottoman Empire, Cambridge Studies in Islamic Civiliẓation*. New York: Cambridge University Press.

And, M. (1963). *A History of Theatre and Popular Entertainment in Turkey*. Ankara: FORUM Yaınları.

Andrews, R. (2014). Resources in Common: Shakespeare and Flaminio Scala. In Henke, R. & Nicholson, E., eds., *Transnational Mobilities in Early Modern Theater*. Farnham: Ashgate, pp. 37–52.

Augel, J. (1971). *Italienische Einwanderung und Wirtschaftstätigkeit in rheinischen Städten des 17. und 18. Jahrhunderts*, Vol. 78 of *Rheinisches Archiv*. Bonn: Ludwig Rührscheid Verlag.

Baldini, U. (2010). Engineering the Mission and Missions as Engineering: Claudio Filippo Grimaldi and his Return to Beijing (1694). In L.F. Barreto, ed., *Tomás Pereira, S.J. (1646–1708): Life, Work and World*. Lisbon: Centro Científico e Cultural de Macau: Fundação para a Ciência e a Tecnologia, pp. 75–184.

Balme, C. B. (2019). *The Globaliẓation of Theatre 1870–1930: The Theatrical Networks of Maurice E. Bandmann*, Cambridge Studies in Modern Theatre. Cambridge: Cambridge University Press.

Baumgarten, A. G. (2018 [1750]). *Ästhetik. Zwei Bände. Band 1: §§ 1–613 / Band 2: §§ 614–904, Einführung, Glossar.* Vol. 572a/B of *Philosophische Bibliothek.* Hamburg: Felix Meiner Verlag.

Beneke, O. (1863). *Von unehrlichen Leuten: Cultur-historische Studien und Geschichten.* Hamburg: Perthes, Besser & Mauke.

Benjamin, W. (2015). *Illuminations.* London: The Bodley Head.

Berensmeyer, I. (2016). From Media Anthropology to Media Ecology. In B. Neumann and A. Nünning, eds., *Travelling Concepts for the Study of Culture.* Berlin: De Gruyter, pp. 321–35.

Bischoff, Erich (1903). *Die Kabbalah: Einführung in die jüdische Mystik und Geheimwissenschaft.* Leipzig: Th. Grieben.

Bloch, M. (1924). *Les rois thaumaturges; étude sur le caractère surnaturel attribué à la puissance royale, particulièrement en France et en Angleterre [. . .].* Strasbourg: Librairie ISTRA.

Bloom, G. (2018). *Gaming the Stage: Playable Media and the Rise of English Commercial Theater.* Ann Arbor: University of Michigan Press.

Bolter, J. D. & Grusin, R. (1999). *Remediation: Understanding New Media.* Cambridge, MA: MIT Press.

Bredekamp, H. (2004). *Die Fenster der Monade: Gottfried Wilhelm Leibniz' Theater der Natur und Kunst.* Vol. XVII of *Acta Humaniora: Schriften zur Kunstwissenschaft und Philosophie.* Berlin: Akademie Verlag.

Brockett, O. G. & Hildy, F. J. (2003). *History of the Theatre.* 9th ed. Boston: Allyn and Bacon.

Brook, P. (1968). *The Empty Space.* London: Penguin.

Brusati, C., ed. (2021). *Samuel van Hoogstraten's Introduction to the Academy of the Painting; or, The Visible World. Translated by Jaap Jacobs.* Los Angeles: Getty Research Centre.

Buccheri, A. (2014). *The Spectacle of Clouds, 1439–1650: Italian Art and Theatre, Visual Culture in Early Modernity.* Burlington, VT: Ashgate.

Burke, P. (2020). *The Polymath: A Cultural History from Leonardo Da Vinci to Susan Sontag*. New Haven, CT: Yale University Press.

Bussels, S. (2012). *Spectacle, Rhetoric and Power: The Triumphal Entry of Prince Philip of Spain Into Antwerp*. Vol. XI of *Ludus – Medieval and Early Renaissance Theatre and Drama*. Amsterdam: Brill | Rodopi. Book.

Butler, A. J. (1909). Calendar of State Papers Foreign: Elizabeth. Vol. 16, May–December 1582. London: His Majesty's Stationery Office. British History Online. https://www.british-history.ac.uk/cal-state-papers/foreign/vol16/.

Butterworth, P. (2005). *Magic on the Early English Stage*. Cambridge: Cambridge University Press.

Butterworth, P. & Normington, K. (2017). *Medieval Theatre Performance: Actors, Dancers, Automata and their Audiences*. Cambridge: D. S. Brewer.

Cabranes-Grant, L. (2016). *From Scenarios to Networks: Performing the Intercultural in Colonial Mexico*. Vol. II of *Performance Works*. Evanston, IL: Northwestern University Press.

Caton, K. E. (2013). The Puppet in Ben Jonson's "Bartholomew Fair". *Early Theatre* 16(1), 51–73.

Chambers, E. K. (2009). *The Elizabethan Stage. 4 vols.* (orig.: 1923). Oxford: Clarendon Press.

Clubb, L. G. (1989). *Italian Drama in Shakespeare's Time*. New Haven, CT: Yale University Press.

Conquergood, D. (2002). Performance Studies: Interventions and Radical Research. *TDR/The Drama Review* 46(2), 145–56.

Crary, J. (1992). *Techniques of the Observer: On Vision and Modernity in the Nineteenth Century (October Books)*. Cambridge, MA: MIT Press.

Das, N., João, Melo, V., Smith, H.Z. & Working, L. (2021). Vagrant/Vagabond. In Das, N., João, Melo, V., Smith, H.Z. & Working, L., eds., *Keywords of Identity, Race, and Human Mobility in Early Modern England*. Amsterdam: Amsterdam University Press, pp. 284–90.

Daston, L. & Park, K. (2012). *Wonders and the Order of Nature, 1150–1750*. New York: Zone Books.

Davies, C. (2023). *What is a Playhouse? England at Play, 1520–1620*. London: Routledge.

Davis, T. C. & Marx, P. W. (2021). On Critical Media History. In Davis, T.C. & Marx, P. W., eds., *The Routledge Companion to Theatre and Performance Historiography*. London: Routledge, pp. 1–39.

Dee, J. (1570). The Mathematicall Praeface to the Elements of Geometrie of Euclid of Megara. In *Elements of Geometrie of Euclid of Megara.*, n.P. London: John Daye.

Dee, J. (2013). The Compendious Rehearsal, etc. In Crossley, J. [et al.] *John Dee's Diary, Catalogue of Manuscripts and Selected Letters*. Cambridge: Cambridge University Press. Original edition, 1842, pp. 111–14.

Del Rio, M. (2000). *Investigations into Magic. Edited and translated by P. G. Maxwell-Stuart*. Manchester: Manchester University Press.

Dessen, A. C. (2009). Stage Directions and the Theater Historian. In Dutton, R., ed., *The Oxford Handbook of Early Modern Theatre*. Oxford: Oxford University Press, pp. 513–27.

Dewitz, B. v. & Nekes, W., eds. (2002). *Ich sehe was, was Du nicht siehst! Sehmaschinen und Bilderwelten: Die Sammlung Werner Nekes*. Göttingen: Steidl.

Eck, C. v. & Bussels, S. (2010). The Visual Arts and the Theatre in Early Modern Europe. *Art History* 33(2): 208–23.

Egan, G. (2016). Playhouses. In Smith, B. R., ed., *Shakespeare's World, 1500–1660*. Vol. I of *The Cambridge Guide to the Worlds of Shakespeare*. Cambridge: Cambridge University Press, pp. 89–95.

Elmentaler, M. & Voeste, A. (2019). Areale Variation im Deutschen historisch: Mittelalter und Frühe Neuzeit. In Herrgen, J. & Schmidt, J. E., eds., *Volume 4: Deutsch*. Vol. IV of *Sprache und Raum:*

Ein internationales Handbuch der Sprachvariation. Berlin: De Gruyter Mouton, pp. 61–100.

Endean, P. (2017). The Spiritual Exercises. In Worcester SJ, T., ed., *The Cambridge Encyclopedia of the Jesuits*. Cambridge: Cambridge University Press, pp. 52–67.

Eversberg, G. (1988). Der Mechanikus Georg Geißelbrecht: Zur Geschichte eines wandernden Marionettentheaters um 1800. In Rudin, B. & Sprengel, P., eds., *Wanderbühne: Theaterkunst als fahrendes Gewerbe*. Berlin: Gesellschaft für Theatergeschichte, pp. 105–28.

Flatt, E. J. (2019). *The Courts of the Deccan Sultanates: Living Well in the Persian Cosmopolis*. Cambridge: Cambridge University Press.

Fleming, A. C. (2017). Letters, Annual. In Worcester SJ, T., ed., *The Cambridge Encyclopedia of the Jesuits*. Cambridge: Cambridge University Press, p. 461 f.

Flores, J. (2007). Distant Wonders: The Strange and the Marvelous between Mughal India and Habsburg Iberia in the Early Seventeenth Century. *Comparative Studies in Society and History* 49(3), 553–81.

Freebury-Jones, D. (2022). *Reading Robert Greene: Recovering Shakespeare's Rival*. New York: Routledge.

Füsslin, G. et al., eds. (1995). *Der Guckkasten: Einblick – Durchblick – Ausblick*. Stuttgart: Füsslin Verlag.

Gitelman, L. (2006). *Always Already New: Media, History, and the Data of Culture*. Cambridge, MA: MIT Press.

Godwin, J. (2009). *Athanasius Kircher's Theatre of the World: The Life and Works of the Last Man to Search for Universal Knowledge*. Rochester, VT: Inner Traditions.

Golvers, N. (2010). F. Verbiest, G. Magalhães, T. Pereyra and the others. The Jesuit Xitang College in Peking (1670–1688) as an extra-ordinary professional milieu. In L.F. Barreto, ed., *Tomás Pereira, S.J. (1646–1708)*:

Life, Work and World. Lisbon: Centro Científico e Cultural de Macau: Fundação para a Ciência e a Tecnologia, pp. 277–98.

Graves, R. B. 2009. Lighting. In Dutton, R., ed. *The Oxford Handbook of Early Modern Theatre*. Oxford: Oxford University Press, pp. 528–42.

Greenblatt, S. (2017). *Marvelous Possessions: The Wonder of the New World. With a New Preface* (orig.: 1991). Chicago: University of Chicago Press.

Guignollet & Séraphin, D. F. (1871). *Le théatre des ombres chinoises nouveau Séraphin des enfants, recueil de jolies pièces amusantes et faciles à monter*. Paris: Le Bailly.

Gunning, T. (1990). The Cinema of Attractions. Early Film, Its Spectator, and the Avant-Garde. In Elsaesser, T. & Barker, A., eds., *Early Cinema: Space, Frame, Narrative*. London: BFI, pp. 56–62.

Guo, L. (2012). *The Performing Arts in Medieval Islam: Shadow Play and Popular Poetry in Ibn Dāniyāl's Mamluk Cairo*. Vol. XCIII of *Islamic History and Civilization: Studies and Texts*. Leiden: Brill.

Habib, I. (2008). *Black Lives in the English Archive, 1500–1677*. Farnham: Ashgate.

Hanser, E.-M. (2020). *Comœdianten und Ordnungsmächte: Frühes deutschsprachiges Berufstheater (1650–1730) im Kontext von Kirche, Staat und Stadt*. Göttingen: Vandenhoeck & Ruprecht.

Hefter, R. (1936). *Die moralische Beurteilung des deutschen Berufsschauspielers*. Emsdetten: Heinr. & J. Lechte.

Heine, C. (1887). *Johannes Velten: Ein Beitrag zur Geschichte des deutschen Theaters im XVII. Jahrhundert*. Halle: E. Karras.

Heise, U. K. (2002). Unnatural Ecologies: The Metaphor of the Environment in Media Theory. *Configurations* 10(1), 149–68.

Henke, R. (2014). The Taming of the Shrew, Italian Intertexts, and Cultural Mobility. In Nicholson, E. & Henke, R., eds., *Transnational Mobilities in Early Modern Theater*. Farnham: Ashgate, pp. 23–36.

Jacob, G. (1925). *Geschichte des Schattentheaters im Morgen- und Abendland*, 2nd rev. ed. Hannover: Orient-Buchhandlung Heinz Lasaire.

Jacob, M. (1938). *Kölner Theater im XVIII. Jahrhundert bis zum Ende der Reichsstädtischen Zeit (1700–1794)*. Emsdetten: Heinr. & J. Lechte.

Jami, C. (2012). *The Emperor's New Mathematics: Western Learning and Imperial Authority During the Kangxi Reign (1662–1722)*. Oxford: Oxford University Press.

Jones, G. (2016). *Shakespeare's Storms*. Manchester: Manchester University Press.

Kaplin, S. (1999). A Puppet Tree: A Model for the Field of Puppet Theatre. *TDR/ The Drama Review* 43(3), 28–35.

Katritzky, M. A. (2005). Reading the Actress in Commedia Imagery. In Brown, P. A. & Parolin, P., ed., *Women Players in England, 1500–1660: Beyond the All-Male Stage*. Aldershot: Ashgate, pp. 109–43.

Katritzky, M. A. (2008). English Troupes in Early Modern Germany: The Women. In Henke, R. & Nicholson, E., eds., *Transnational Exchange in Early Modern Theater*, Vol. II of *Studies in Performance and Early Modern Drama*. Aldershot: Ashgate, pp. 35–46.

Katritzky, M. A. & Drábek, P., eds. (2020). *Transnational Connections in Early Modern Theatre*. Manchester: Manchester University Press.

Keating, J. (2018). *Animating Empire: Automata, the Holy Empire, and the Early Modern World*. University Park: Pennsylvania State University Press.

Khan, I. A. (1996). Coming of Gunpowder to the Islamic World and North India: Spotlight on the Role of the Mongols. *Journal of Asian History* 30 (1), 27–45.

Kittler, F. (2011). *Optische Medien: Berliner Vorlesung 1999*. Berlin: Merve Verlag.

Kleutghen, K. (2015a). *Imperial Illusions: Crossing Pictorial Boundaries in the Qing Palaces*. Seattle: University of Washington Press.

Kleutghen, K. (2015b). Peepboxes, Society, and Visuality in Early Modern China. *Art History* 38(38), 762–77.

Kodera, S. (2012). Giambattista della Porta's Histrionic Science. *California Italian Studies* 3(1), 1–27.

Korda, N. (2011). *Labors Lost: Women's Work and the Early Modern English Stage*. Philadelphia: University of Pennsylvania Press.

Korda, N. (2021). Gyno Ludens: A Doll House Redux. In Davis, T.C. & Marx, P. W., eds., *The Routledge Companion to Theatre and Performance Historiography*. London: Routledge, pp. 65–85.

Koslofsky, C. (2011). *Evening's Empire: A History of the Night in Early Modern Europe, New Studies in European History*. Cambridge: Cambridge University Press.

Lavin, I. (1964). Review: Fontana di Trevi, Commedia inedita by Gian Lorenzo Bernini and Cesare d'Onofrio. *The Art Bulletin* 46(4), 568–72.

Lavin, I. (2007). *Visible Spirit: The Art of Gianlorenzo Bernini. Vol. 1*. London: Pindar Press.

Lazardzig, J. & Rößler, H. (2016). Technologies of Theatre: Joseph Furttenbach and the Transfer of Mechanical Knowledge in Early Modern Theatre Cultures. *Zeitsprünge, Forschungen zur Frühen Neuzeit* 20(3–4), 271–309.

Lehmann, H.-T. (2006). *Postdramatic Theatre*. London: Routledge.

Lehner, U. L. (2016). *The Catholic Enlightenment: The Forgotten History of a Global Movement*. Oxford: Oxford University Press.

Lezra, J. (2014). Trade in Exile. In Nicholson, E. & Henke, R., eds., *Transnational Mobilities in Early Modern Theater*. Farnham: Ashgate, pp. 199–216.

Lipton, L. (2021). *The Cinema in Flux: The Evolution of Motion Picture Technology from the Magic Lantern to the Digital Era*. New York: Springer Nature.

Malayail, A. (2016). Veṭikkampavishi: A Malayam Text on Pyrotechny. *Indian Journal of History of Science* 51(4), 613–29.

Mannoni, L. (2000). *The Great Art of Light and Shadow: Archaeology of the Cinem.* Exeter: University of Exeter Press.

Mannoni, L., Nekes, W. & Warner, M., eds. (2004). *Eyes, Lies and Illusions: Drawn from the Nekes Collection.* London: Hayward Gallery.

Marx, P. W. (2019). Between Metaphor and Cultural Practices: *Theatrum* And *Scena* in the German-Speaking Sphere before 1648. In Penskaya, E. & Küpper, J., ed., *Theater as Metaphor.* Berlin: De Gruyter, pp. 11–29.

Marx, P. W. (2021a). On Circulation and Recycling. In Davis, T.C. & Marx, P. W., eds., *The Routledge Companion to Theatre and Performance Historiography.* London: Routledge, pp. 327–47.

Marx, P. W. (2021b). "Turtles all the way down." Zu methodischen Fragen der Theaterhistoriographie. *Forum Modernes Theater* 32(2), 5–22.

Mayer-Deutsch, A. (2014). The Ideal Musaeum Kircherianum and the *Ignatian Exercitia spiritualia.* In Lazardzig, J., Schramm, H. & Schwarte, L., eds., *Theatrum Scientiarum – English Edition. Instruments in Art and Science; On the Architectonics of Cultural Boundaries in the 17th Century.* Berlin: De Gruyter, pp. 235–56.

McEvoy, S. (2008). *Ben Jonson, Renaissance Dramatist.* Edinburgh: Edinburgh University Press.

McLuhan, M. (2009). *Understanding Media: The Extensions of Man.* Abingdon: Routledge.

Milano, A. (2016). *Martin Engelbrecht: Perspektivtheater – Dioramen.* Stuttgart: Füsslin.

Minissale, G. (2007). A Short History of Anti-Illusionism. In Minissale, G. & Jeffery, C., ed., *Global and Local Art Histories.* Newcastle: Cambridge Scholars, pp. 117–44.

Moreh, S. (1992). *Live Theatre and Dramatic Literature in the Medieval Arab World.* Edinburgh: Edinburgh University Press.

Mottahedeh, R. P. (1997). Ajā'ib in the Thousand and One Nights. In Hovannisian, R.G. & Sabagh, G., eds., *The Thousand and One Nights in Arabic Literature and Society*. Cambridge: Cambridge University Press.

Needham, J. (1962). *Physics and Physical Technology*. Vol. IV of *Science and Civilisation in China*. Cambridge: Cambridge University Press.

Needham, J. (1985). *Gunpowder as the Fourth Power, East and West: First East Asian History of Science Foundation Lecture, Presented at the University of Hong Kong, 20 October 1983*. Hong Kong: Hong Kong University Press.

Nekes, W. & Kienninger, E., eds. (2015). *Kinomagie: Was geschah ʒwischen den Bildern. Die Sammlung Werner Nekes*. Vienna: verlag filmarchiv austria.

Niessen, C. (1919). *Studien ʒur Geschichte des Jesuiten-Dramas in Köln*. Cologne: Universitäre Habilitationsschrift.

Niessen, C. (1940). *Frau Magister Velten verteidigt die Schaubühne: [Schriften aus der Kampfʒeit des deutschen Nationaltheaters]; Erneuert ʒum 50. Geburtstage des Präsidenten der Reichstheaterkammer Ludwig Körner*. Cologne.

Orgel, S. (2002). *The Authentic Shakespeare and Other Problems of the Early Modern Stage*. London: Routledge.

Osterhammel, J. (2018). *Unfabling the East: The Enlightenment's Encounter with Asia*. Princeton, NJ: Princeton University Press.

Parikka, J. (2012). *What Is Media Archaeology?* Cambridge: Polity.

Paul, M. (2011). *Reichsstadt und Schauspiel: Theatrale Kunst im Nürnberg des 17. Jahrhunderts*. Tübingen: Max Niemeyer. https://doi.org/10.1515/9783110935271.

Pies, E. (1970). Carl Andreas Paulsen und die ersten deutschen Berufsschauspieler: Zur Genealogie der Wandertruppen in Deutschland. In Pies, E., ed., *Otto C. A. Zur Nedden. Festgabe ʒum 68. Geburtstag*. Bensberg-Frankenforst: [private], pp. 59–65.

Pratt, M. L. (1992). *Imperial Eyes: Travel Writing and Transculturation*. London: Routledge.

Proschan, F. (1983). The Semiotic Study of Puppets, Masks, and Performing Objects... *Semiotica* 47(1/4), 3–44.

Purschke, H. R. (1979). *Die Anfänge der Puppenspielformen und ihre vermutlichen Ursprünge*. Bochum: Deutsches Institut für Puppenspiel.

Purschke, H. R. (1980). *Puppenspiel und verwandte Künste in der Freien Reichs-Stadt Frankfurt am Main*. Frankfurt/Main: Puppenspielzentrum Frankfurt am Main.

Purschke, H. R. (1981). Puppenspiel und verwandte Künste in der Reichsstadt Nürnberg. *Mitteilungen des Vereins für Geschichte der Stadt Nürnberg* 68(68), 221–59.

Reilly, K. (2011). *Automata and Mimesis on the Stage of Theatre History*. Basingstoke: Palgrave Macmillan.

Roach, J. (1996). *Cities of the Dead: Circum-Atlantic Performance, The Social Foundations of Aesthetic Forms*. New York: Columbia University Press.

Robinson, A. (2006). *The Last Men Who Knew Everything*. New York: Pi Press.

Roller, H.U. (1965). *Der Nürnberger Schembartlauf*. Vol. XI of *Studien zum Fest- und Maskenwesen des späten Mittelalters, Volksleben*. Tübingen: Tübinger Vereinigung für Volkskunde.

Rotger, N., Roig-Sanz, D. & Puxan-Oliva, M. (2019). Introduction: Towards a Cross-Disciplinary History of the Global in the Humanities and the Social Sciences. *Journal of Global History* 14(3):325–34.

Rudin, B. (2004). *Lebenselixier: Theater, Budenzauber, Freilichtspektakel im Alten Reich*. Reichenbach im Vogtland: Neuberin-Museum.

Sager, J. (2013). *The Aesthetics of Spectacle in Early Modern Drama and Modern Cinema: Robert Greene's Theatre of* Attraction. Houndmills: Palgrave Macmillan.

Santos, B. d. S. (2007). Beyond Abyssal Thinking: From Global Lines to Ecologies of Knowledges. *Review (Fernand Braudel Center)* 30(1), 45–89.

Santos, B. d. S. (2018). *The End of the Cognitive Empire: The Coming of Age of Epistemologies of the South*. Durham, NC: Duke University Press.

Savarese, N. (2010). *Eurasian Theatre: Drama and Performance Between East and West from Classical Antiquity to the Present*. Holstebro: Icarus.

Scheeben, H. C. (1932). *Albertus Magnus*. Bonn: Verlag der Buchgemeinde.

Scheitler, I. (2017). Die Verthönung: Illustration auf dem Theater. In Robert, J., ed., *Intermedialität in der Frühen Neuzeit: Formen, Funktionen, Konzepte*. Berlin: De Gruyter, pp. 21–38.

Schneider, R. (2011). *Performing Remains: Art and War in Times of Theatrical Reenactment*. London: Routledge.

Shea SJ H. (2017). Indifference. In Worcester SJ, T., ed., *The Cambridge Encyclopedia of the Jesuits*. Cambridge: Cambridge University Press, p. 392 f.

Singh, Kavita. (2017). *Real Birds in Imagined Gardens: Mughal Painting between Persia and Europe, Getty Research Institute Council Lecture*. Los Angeles: Getty Publication.

Sittig, Claudius. (2012). Kulturelle Zentren der Frühen Neuzeit. Perspektiven der Interdisziplinären Forschung. In Adam, W. & Westphal, S., eds., *Handbuch Kultureller Zentren der Frühen Neuzeit: Städte und Residenzen im alten deutschen Sprachraum*. Berlin: De Gruyter, pp. XXXI–LV.

Sluhovsky, M. (2017). *Becoming a New Self: Practices of Belief in Early Modern Catholicism*. Chicago: University of Chicago Press.

Standaert SJ, N. (2017a). China. In Worcester SJ, T., ed., *The Cambridge Encyclopedia of the Jesuits*. Cambridge: Cambridge University Press, pp. 160–5.

Standaert SJ N. (2017b). Chinese Rites Controversy. In Worcester SJ, T., ed., *The Cambridge Encyclopedia of the Jesuits*. Cambridge: Cambridge University Press, p. 165 f.

Stern, T. (2013). "If I could see the Puppets Dallying": Der Bestrafte Brudermord and Hamlet's Encounter with the Puppets. *Shakespeare Bulletin* 31(3), 337–52.

Subrahmanyam, S. (1997). Connected Histories: Notes Towards a Reconfiguration of Early Modern Eurasia. *Modern Asian Studies* 31(3), 735–62.

Subrahmanyam, S. (2012). *Courtly Encounters: Translating Courtliness and Violence in Early Modern Eurasia.* Cambridge, MA: Harvard University Press.

Subrahmanyam, S. (2019). *Empires between Islam & Christianity, 1500–1800.* Albany: State University of New York.

Tardel, H. (1926). Zur Bremischen Theatergeschichte (1563–1763). *Bremisches Jahrbuch* 30(30), 263–310.

Taubert, T. S. (2018). *Die Szene des Wunderbaren: Die Shakespeare-Elfen im Wechselspiel von Musik und Maschine.* Vol. II of *Szene & Horizont: Theaterwissenschaftliche Studien.* Stuttgart: J. B. Metzler.

Taylor, D. (2003). *The Archive and the Repertoire: Performing Cultural Memory in the Americas.* Durham, NC: Duke University Press.

Tebra, W. (1982). The Magic Lantern of Giovanni Da Fontana. *New Magic Lantern Journal* 2(2), 10–11.

Terzioğlu, D. (1995). The Imperial Circumcision Festival of 1582: An Interpretation. *Muqarnas* 12(12), 84–100.

Tkaczyk, V. (2011). *Himmels-Falten: Zur Theatralität des Fliegens in der Frühen Neuzeit.* München: Fink.

Tripps, J. (2000). *Das handelnde Bildwerk in der Gotik. Forschungen zu den Bedeutungsschichten und der Funktion des Kirchengebäudes und seiner Ausstattung in der Hoch- und Spätgotik,* 2nd ed. Berlin: Gebr. Mann.

Truitt, E. R. (2015). *Medieval Robots: Mechanism, Magic, Nature, and Art.* Philadelphia: University of Pennsylvania Press.

Vanhaelen, A. (2022). *The Moving Statues of Seventeenth-Century Amsterdam: Automata, Waxworks, Fountains, Labyrinths.* University Park: Pennsylvania State University Press.

Vaughan, V. M. & Vaughan, A. T. (1999). Introduction. In Vaughan, V. M. & Vaughan, A. T., eds., *William Shakespeare: The Tempest. The Arden Shakespeare*. London: Bloomsbury.

Wagenaar, W. A., Wagenaar-Fischer, M. & Duller, A. (2014). Dutch Lantern Workshops. In Wagenaar, W. A., Wagenaar-Fischer, M. & Duller, A., eds., *Dutch Perspectives: 350 Years of Visual Entertainment Based on the Research of Willem Albert Wagenaar and Annet Duller*. London: Magic Lantern Society, pp. 27–53.

Warburg, A. (2010). Heidnisch-antike Weissagung in Wort und Bild zu Luthers Zeiten. In Treml, M. & Weigel, S., eds., *Werke in einem Band*. Berlin: Suhrkamp, pp. 424–91.

Warde, P. (2006). *Ecology, Economy and State Formation in Early Modern Germany*. Cambridge: Cambridge University Press.

Warner, M. (2004). Camera Lucida. In Mannoni, L., Nekes, W. & Warner, M., eds., *Eyes, Lies and Illusions: Drawn from the Nekes Collection*. London: Hayward Gallery, pp. 13–23.

Warner, M. (2006). *Phantasmagoria: Spirit Visions, Metaphors, and Media into the Twenty-First Century*. Oxford: Oxford University Press.

Warner, M. (2011). *Stranger Magic: Charmed States and the Arabian Nights*. Cambridge, MA: Harvard University Press.

Warwick, G. (2012). *Bernini: Art as Theatre*. New Haven, CT: Yale University Press.

Weimann, R. (1978). *Shakespeare and the Popular Tradition in the Theater: Studies in the Social Function of Dramatic Form and Function*. Baltimore: Johns Hopkins University Press.

Weimann, R. & Bruster, D. (2008). *Shakespeare and the Power of Performance: Stage and Page in the Elizabethan Theatre*. Cambridge: Cambridge University Press.

Werret, S. (2010). *Fireworks: Pyrotechnic Arts and Sciences in European History*. Chicago: University of Chicago Press.

West, W. N. (2013). Chapter 8: Intertheatricality. In Turner, H.S., ed., *Early Modern Theatricality*. Oxford: Oxford University Press, pp. 151–72.

West, W. N. (2021). *Common Understandings, Poetic Confusion: Playhouses and Playgoers in Elizabethan England*. Chicago: University of Chicago Press.

Wiener, P. P. (1940). Leibniz's Project of a Public Exhibition of Scientific Inventions. *Journal of the History of Ideas* 1(2), 232–40.

Wishnitzer, A. (2021). *As Night Falls: Eighteenth-Century Ottoman Cities after Dark*. Cambridge: Cambridge University Press.

Worthen, W. B. (2003). *Shakespeare and the Force of Modern Performance*. Cambridge: Cambridge University Press.

Worthen, W. B. (2010). *Drama: Between Poetry and Performance*. Chichester, UK: Wiley-Blackwell.

Worthen, W. B. (2014). *Shakespeare Performance Studies*. Cambridge: Cambridge University Press.

Wynants, N. (2019). Media-Archaeological Approaches to Theatre and Performance: An Introduction. In Wynants, N., ed., *Media Archaeology and Intermedial Performance. Deep Time of the Theatre*. Cham: Palgrave Macmillan, pp. 1–19.

Yates, F. (2002). *Giordano Bruno and the Hermetic Tradition*. London: Routledge

Yates, F. A. (2001). *The Occult Philosophy in the Elizabethan Age*. London: Routledge.

Zadeh, T. (2023). *Wonders and Rarities: The Marvelous Book that Traveled the World and Mapped the Cosmos*. Cambridge, MA: Harvard University Press.

Zambelli, P. (2007). *White Magic, Black Magic in the European Renaissance: From Ficino, Pico, della Porta to Trithemius, Agrippa, Bruno*. Leiden: Brill.

Zielinski, S. (2008). *Deep Time of the Media: Toward an Archaeology of Hearing and Seeing by Technical Means*. Cambridge, MA: MIT Press.

Acknowledgments

The questions addressed in this volume have accompanied me for a long time. More encounters and conversations than I can count have contributed to its evolution. While painfully aware that I will not be able to do justice to all of these, I want to mention some of my companions on this path.

Among my academic interlocutors, I would like to highlight Tracy C. Davis, with whom I have developed a long-standing discussion of historiographical questions, archival adventures, and the pleasure and urgency of developing new forms of telling histories.

Ruthie Abeliovich, Sharon Aronson-Lehavi, Leo Cabranes-Grant, Pavel Drábek, Erith Jaffe-Berg, and Odai Johnson have shared many of these discussions. Bishnupriya Dutt, Indu Jain, and Ameet Parameswaran have deepened my understanding of a historiographic perspective that opens its horizon beyond the stereotypical Western narrative. Habbo Knoch has been a constant challenging and encouraging presence in this attempt. Stephan Ch. Kessler SJ is a generous interlocutor in questions of early modern religion and Ignatian spirituality.

My colleagues in Cologne, particularly at the Theaterwissenschaftliche Sammlung (TWS), have been indispensable for the development of this book. My thanks go to Mathilde Frank, Gerald Köhler, Nora Probst, and Enes Türkoğlu – representing also the wonderful team at the TWS. I am especially grateful for the generous help of Anna-Lu Rausch and Sophie Totz.

Jessica Hinds-Bond has assisted me in bringing this book to life in form and language – exemplarily kind and indispensable at the same time.

As a series editor, William Worthen has been supportive and encouraging throughout the entire process.

Special thanks go to my daughters, Miriam and Rebecca, who have taught me new dimensions of marvels and wonder.

I dedicate this book – as a fragmentary sign of my gratitude and affection – to T. Sofie Taubert, my companion and fellow wonder-seeker.

Cambridge Elements ☰

Shakespeare Performance

W. B. Worthen
Barnard College

W. B. Worthen is Alice Brady Pels Professor in the Arts and Chair
of the Theatre Department at Barnard College. He is also co-chair
of the Ph.D. Program in Theatre at Columbia University, where
he is Professor of English and Comparative Literature.

About the Series

Shakespeare Performance is a dynamic collection in a field that is both always emerging and always evanescent. Responding to the global range of Shakespeare performance today, the series launches provocative, urgent criticism for researchers, graduate students, and practitioners. Publishing scholarship with a direct bearing on the contemporary contexts of Shakespeare performance, it considers specific performances, material and social practices, ideological and cultural frameworks, emerging and significant artists, and performance histories.

Cambridge Elements ≡

Shakespeare Performance

Printed in the United States
by Baker & Taylor Publisher Services